TAITTIRĪYA

Translated with notes based on Śaṅkara's commentary

SWAMI LOKESWARANANDA

RAMAKRISHNA MISSION INSTITUTE OF CULTURE
Gol Park, Kolkata 700 029

Published by
Swami Suparnananda, Secretary,
Ramakrishna Mission Institute of Culture
Kolkata-700 029, India

First Published in January 1996
Fifth Print in July 2020 : 2,000
Total Impression : 8,050

Price : Rupees Seventy only

ISBN : 81-85843-75-9

Printed at
Computer typeset at Ramakrishna Mission Institute of Culture
Photo-offset at
A. G. Printers
Kolkata 700 009

PUBLISHER'S NOTE

This edition of the Taittirīya Upaniṣad is based on Swami Lokeswarananda's weekly discourses. It is the eighth in a series of Upaniṣads being published by the Institute. Readers will find this Upaniṣad simple and lucid. It is also authentic in that it follows Śaṅkara's interpretation.

January 1996

KEY TO TRANSLITERATION AND PRONUNCIATION

		Sounds like			Sounds like
अ	a	o in s*o*n	ड	ḍ	d
आ	ā	a in m*a*ster	ढ	ḍh	dh in go*dh*ood
इ	i	i in *i*f	ण	ṇ	n in u*n*der
ई	ī	ee in f*ee*l	त	t	French t
उ	u	u in f*u*ll	थ	th	th in *th*umb
ऊ	ū	oo in b*oo*t	द	d	th in *th*en
ऋ	ṛ	somewhat between r and ri	ध	dh	theh in brea*the h*ere
ए	e	a in ev*a*de	न	n	n
ऐ	ai	y in m*y*	प	p	p
ओ	o	o in *o*ver	फ	ph	ph in loo*p-h*ole
औ	au	ow in n*ow*	ब	b	b
क	k	k	भ	bh	bh in a*bh*or
ख	kh	ckh in blo*ckh*ead	म	m	m
ग	g	g (hard)	य	y	y
घ	gh	gh in lo*g-h*ut	र	r	r
ङ	ṅ	ng	ल	l	l
च	c	ch (not k)	व	v	v in a*v*ert
छ	ch	chh in cat*ch h*im	श	ś	sh
ज	j	j	ष	ṣ	sh in *sh*ow
झ	jh	dgeh in he*dgeh*og	स	s	s
ञ	ñ	n (somewhat)	ह	h	h
ट	ṭ	t	.	ṁ	m in hu*m*
ठ	ṭh	th in an*t-h*ill	:	ḥ	half h in hu*h*!

INVOCATION

ॐ शं नो मित्रः शं वरुणः। शं नो भवत्वर्यमा। शं न इन्द्रो बृहस्पतिः। शं नो विष्णुरुरुक्रमः। नमो ब्रह्मणे। नमस्ते वायो। त्वमेव प्रत्यक्षं ब्रह्मासि। त्वामेव प्रत्यक्षं ब्रह्म वदिष्यामि। ऋतं वदिष्यामि। सत्यं वदिष्यामि। तन्मामवतु। तद्वक्तारमवतु। अवतु माम्। अवतु वक्तारम्।

ॐ शान्तिः शान्तिः शान्तिः॥

Om. Śaṁ no mitraḥ śaṁ varuṇaḥ; Śaṁ no bhavatvaryamā; Śaṁ na indro bṛhaspatiḥ: Śaṁ no viṣṇururukramaḥ; Namo brahmaṇe; Namaste vāyo; Tvameva pratyakṣaṁ brahmāsi; Tvāmeva pratyakṣaṁ brahma vadiṣyāmi; Ṛtaṁ vadiṣyāmi; Satyaṁ vadiṣyāmi; Tanmāmavatu; Tadvaktāramavatu; Avatu mām; Avatu vaktāram. Om Śāntiḥ Śāntiḥ Śāntiḥ.

ॐ सह नाववतु। सह नौ भुनक्तु। सह वीर्यं करवावहै। तेजस्वि नावधीतमस्तु मा विद्विषावहै।

ॐ शान्तिः शान्तिः शान्तिः॥

Om. Saha nāvavatu; Saha nau bhunaktu; Saha vīryaṁ karavāvahai; Tejasvi nāvadhītamastu mā vidviṣāvahai. Om Śāntiḥ Śāntiḥ Śāntiḥ.

(For translations see verse I.i.1 and the introduction to Part II.)

TAITTIRĪYA UPANIṢAD

The Taittirīya Upaniṣad is included in the Kṛṣṇa (Black) Yajur Veda. The word *taittirīya* is derived from *tittiri*, which means 'partridge.' There is a story behind this name: Once Yājñavalkya offended his teacher, Vaiśampāyana. Yājñavalkya was a very intelligent young man, much advanced in scholarship, but because of his pride his teacher became angry and said to him: 'I have taught you so much. Surrender it all to me now. You have to return it.' So Yājñavalkya vomitted out all the knowledge that he had acquired from Vaiśampāyana.

Now this knowledge was very sacred, very precious. Since it could not go to waste, Vaiśampāyana said to his other disciples, 'Swallow this knowledge that is here on the ground.' The other disciples were then temporarily transformed into partridges and swallowed it. Probably the idea behind the story is that knowledge is always pure, and as knowledge of the Self is the purest of all, it should never be neglected. It should be acquired by any means.

The Yajur Veda has two parts—Kṛṣṇa and Śukla. The word *kṛṣṇa* means black, or impure. Knowledge is never impure, but a receptacle (*āśraya*) of knowledge—that is, a person who disseminates knowledge—may be impure. Knowledge coming from such a person never serves any purpose. Here, the knowledge which the partridges (i.e., the other disciples of Vaiśampāyana) picked up is described as impure, because the disciples themselves were impure. Yājñavalkya, however, was an exceptional person. In order to re-acquire knowledge of the Vedas, he worshipped the sun and became as bright and pure as the sun. The knowledge that he acquired then is described as *śukla,* white.

This Upaniṣad is divided into three parts, called *vallīs.* The first part is called *Śīkṣā-vallī,* and it mainly deals with pronunciation and phonetics. In those days students were taught the proper way to chant the Vedic texts. This was considered very important because if the chanting and pronunciation were not done correctly, the meaning might change. But this section also gives details about how you should pray: how you should direct your eyes, how and where you should place your legs, and so on. If you pray the way the Upaniṣad tells you, you will then be rewarded with children, money, heaven, and even Self-knowledge. Here the stress is on discipline of both the body and the mind. Given the right kind of body and mind, you can achieve everything you like.

The Śīkṣā-vallī also praises the worship of Om, for Om is the symbol of Brahman. But, it is not only that—it is also the connecting link between one thing and another in the world. It thereby sustains the world. The worship of Om brings you both affluence and intellectual eminence, and with these you are able to attract students from every quarter. The vallī also recommends other modes of worship mentioned in the Vedas, the purpose of each being the attainment of Self-knowledge.

This vallī has altogether eleven sections, each one dedicated to a most enlightening discussion by Śaṅkara on how you can prepare yourself for knowledge. In the course of the discussions many issues are raised and debated, the most important of which is the place of work vis-à-vis knowledge. The conclusion reached is that knowledge is something independent and not something created. Nonetheless, you have to perform duties prescribed by the scriptures.

There are also some moral principles discussed, from which you should never deviate. Chief among them are truthfulness and righteousness. As a householder you must also respect your parents and teachers, welcome guests, and treat them with due respect. You are also told to help others, but you are cautioned that in doing so you must not show any disrespect to those whom you are helping.

Another conclusion which emerges from the discussion is that Self-knowledge is open to all, irrespective of who you are and what you are. All that is needed is that you acquire the requisite amount of self-discipline. It is this self-discipline that then gives the purity of mind which precedes Self-knowledge.

The last instructions on moral principles are given to the students who have finished their studies and are ready to return home. Even now, in some universities, these same instructions are given to the out-going students.

The second part of the Upaniṣad is called *Brahmānanda-vallī*. *Brahmānanda* means 'the bliss of Brahman,' the bliss that you enjoy when you know you are nothing but Brahman. This Brahman is our inmost Self, but we are not conscious of the fact because the Self is hidden under several layers, or sheaths, called *kośas*. It is like a sword hidden in its sheath. We have to remove these sheaths and discover the Self.

What are these sheaths? The first is the sheath made up of food (*anna*), or matter. It is the grossest. The next is the sheath of the vital breath (*prāṇa*). The third is the sheath of the mind (*manas*). The fourth is that of the intellect (*vijñāna*). The fifth and last is called the sheath of bliss (*ānanda*). These sheaths are arranged from gross to fine, one inside the other. They are really levels of consciousness, the highest of them being the level where one enjoys the bliss of Brahman. The goal of life is to go beyond all levels—to reach a state where one loses one's separate identity in Brahman.

The Upaniṣad discusses how these sheaths appear real to us—so real, in fact, that we think we are the sheaths. But the beauty of this Upaniṣad is that it does not say to deny the sheaths. The Upaniṣad says that you cannot afford to neglect even your body. You should treat everything as Brahman—even what is gross, what is material. The body is also Brahman. It is Brahman in the sense that it is a reflection of Brahman. And it is a gateway to Self-knowledge. If you do not have a sound, healthy body, how can you make any spiritual progress?

Similarly, you have to have a sound mind and a sharp intellect. All these things—the body, the organs, and the mind—are tools. They may harm us sometimes, but they may also do much good, depending on how we use them. But we must have them to attain Self-knowledge.

The message of the Brahmānanda-vallī is that if you know Brahman you become Brahman yourself, and you also attain the highest. Brahman is described as *satyam* (Truth), *jñānam* (Knowledge), and *anantam* (Infinity). Are these words used as qualifying words? No. You would use such qualifying words if you were going to separate one Brahman from many other Brahmans. But you are describing the same Brahman, which is *satyam, jñānam,* and *anantam* at the same time. What is meant is that Brahman is *satyam,* Brahman is *jñānam,* and Brahman is also *anantam.*

The scriptures also say that Brahman is the Self of all. This conclusion is drawn from the fact that all that exists is derived from Brahman. Brahman is without name and form. And it is the same Brahman that is at one point the knower, at another point the known, and yet at another point knowledge. Only Brahman can be all these three at the same time. In short, Brahman is everything, and everything is Brahman.

This vallī also poses several questions challenging the validity of the Vedāntic point of view. Take, for instance, the Vedāntic theory that the creator creates something and having created it, then enters into it. How is that possible? The Vedāntic answer is that as the Self is everywhere and in everything, the creation by the Self and the entry of the Self into that which is created are both illusory. It is to be remembered that the Self is the inmost being of everything.

In this Upaniṣad we find that these kośas, or sheaths, are being praised. This is done in the third part, the Bhṛgu-vallī, through a story. A sage named Varuṇa had a son who must have been a very thoughtful boy. One day the son, Bhṛgu, came to his father and asked to be taught about Brahman. As a good teacher knows that he cannot teach everything at once, so Varuṇa led Bhṛgu step by step to the realization of Brahman.

At first Varuṇa told his son that Brahman is the source of everything and asked him to meditate. Bhṛgu thought his father was saying that this physical universe is Brahman. His father did not contradict him, but asked him to go on meditating. Bhṛgu continued to meditate and finally discovered that Brahman is not only the source of this physical universe, but also of the vital breath, the mind, the intellect, and bliss. Indeed, Brahman alone is real and everything else is merely superimposed on it.

PART ONE
ŚĪKṢĀ-VALLĪ

Chapter One

ॐ शं नो मित्रः शं वरुणः। शं नो भवत्वर्यमा। शं न इन्द्रो बृहस्पतिः। शं नो विष्णुरुरुक्रमः। नमो ब्रह्मणे। नमस्ते वायो। त्वमेव प्रत्यक्षं ब्रह्मासि। त्वामेव प्रत्यक्षं ब्रह्म वदिष्यामि। ऋतं वदिष्यामि। सत्यं वदिष्यामि। तन्मामवतु। तद्वक्तारमवतु। अवतु माम्। अवतु वक्तारम्। ॐ शान्तिः शान्तिः शान्तिः॥ १॥ इति प्रथमोऽनुवाकः॥

Om. Śaṁ no mitraḥ śaṁ varuṇaḥ; Śaṁ no bhavatvaryamā; Śaṁ na indro bṛhaspatiḥ; Śaṁ no viṣṇururukramaḥ; Namo brahmaṇe; Namaste vāyo; Tvameva pratyakṣaṁ brahmāsi; Tvāmeva pratyakṣaṁ brahma vadiṣyāmi; Ṛtaṁ vadiṣyāmi; Satyaṁ vadiṣyāmi; Tanmāmavatu; Tadvaktāramavatu; Avatu mām; Avatu vaktāram. Om Śāntiḥ Śāntiḥ Śāntiḥ. Iti prathamo-'nuvākaḥ.

Mitraḥ, Mitra, the sun; *naḥ,* to us; *śam,* [be] propitious; *varuṇaḥ,* Varuṇa, the deity governing the downward breath and also night; *śam,* [be] propitious [to us]; *aryamā,* Aryaman, the deity governing the eyes and the sun; *bhavatu,* be; *śam,* propitious; *naḥ,* to us; *indraḥ,* Indra, the deity symbolizing strength; *bṛhaspatiḥ,* Bṛhaspati, the deity symbolizing speech and the intellect; *naḥ śam,* [be] propitious to us; *viṣṇuḥ urukramaḥ,* Viṣṇu, who walks with long strides and symbolizes strength; *naḥ śam,* [be] propitious to us; *brahmane namaḥ,* salutations to Brahman [as]; *vāyo namah te,* Vāyu, salutations to you; *tvam eva pratyakṣam brahma asi,* you are no other than Brahman; *tvām eva pratyakṣam brahma vadiṣyāmi,* I will declare that you are truly Brahman; *ṛtam vadiṣyāmi,* I will declare you as righteousness itself; *satyam vadiṣyāmi,* I will declare you [also] as Truth; *tat mām avatu,* may that [Brahman] protect me; *tat vaktāram avatu,* may that [Brahman] protect the speaker [teacher]; *avatu mām,* may [Brahman] protect me; *avatu vaktāram,* may [Brahman] protect the speaker [teacher]; *śāntiḥ,* peace [at the level of one's own body and mind, *ādhyātmika*]; *śāntiḥ,* peace [at the level of the elements, *ādhidaivika*]; *śāntiḥ,* peace [at the level of the animals, *ādhibhautika*]. *Iti prathamaḥ anuvākaḥ,* here ends the first chapter.

1. May Mitra, the Sun, be propitious to us. May Varuṇa be propitious to us. May Aryaman be propitious to us. May Indra be propitious to us. May Bṛhaspati be propitious to us. May Viṣṇu, who walks with long strides, be propitious to us. Salutations to Brahman. Salutations to you, O Vāyu. You are no other than Brahman. I will declare that you are truly Brahman. I will declare that you are righteousness itself. I will declare that you are Truth. May Brahman as Vāyu protect me. May he protect the speaker. May he

protect me. May he protect the speaker. Peace! Peace! Peace!

This is a prayer to various deities. We are going to begin a very hard task. The study of Vedānta is the most difficult, but at the same time the most covetable, undertaking, so we need the blessings, good wishes, and support of all the deities. *Śam* means 'be propitious,' 'be kind,' 'be helpful.'

Mitra and Varuṇa are two of the gods. The sun is often referred to as Mitra, so he is considered to be the god of the day. Varuṇa is the deity of the night. Aryaman is the god who controls the entire solar system and also the eyes. Viṣṇu is called *urukramaḥ,* he who takes long strides. The deities in the hymn go from small to big. Viṣṇu is vast—bigger than Varuṇa or Mitra.

Vāyu, the god of air, is an important deity. He is everywhere, so he is called here *Brahman.* The word *brahman* means *bṛhat-tama,* the biggest. The Upaniṣad says here that Vāyu is a symbol of Brahman, and that he is *pratyakṣam,* perceptible. He is direct. He can be felt.

The words *ṛtam* and *satyam* have almost the same meaning, but there is a slight difference. *Ṛtam* means 'the moral order.' It is righteousness, or moral principles. No society or civilization—not even the universe—can be sustained without *ṛtam,* without a moral order. *Satyam* means 'truth.' The student says: 'I will call you the moral order. I will call you Truth.'

Tat mām avatu tat vaktāram avatu. 'Please look after

me. Please look after the teacher also.' Both the teacher and the student must be physically and mentally in good shape. If the student is dull, he cannot learn; and if the teacher is dull, he cannot teach. So both of them have to be intellectually fit, physically fit, and spiritually fit.

Śāntiḥ Śāntiḥ Śāntiḥ. There are three sources of trouble for a human being: his own body and mind, the elements, and animals. These three sources in Sanskrit are *ādhyātmika, ādhidaivika,* and *ādhibhautika.* The word 'peace' is said three times in the prayer so that there may be no trouble from any of these three sources.

Chapter Two

ॐ शीक्षां व्याख्यास्यामः। वर्णः स्वरः। मात्रा बलम्। साम सन्तानः। इत्युक्तः शीक्षाध्यायः॥ १॥ इति द्वितीयोऽनुवाकः॥

Om. Śīkṣāṁ vyākhyāsyāmaḥ; Varṇaḥ svaraḥ; Mātrā balam; Sāma santānaḥ; Ityuktaḥ śīkṣādhyāyaḥ. Iti dvitīyo'nuvākaḥ.

Śīkṣām, pronunciation; *vyākhyāsyāmaḥ,* we will explain; *varṇaḥ,* the sound of the letters; *svaraḥ,* modulations of the voice; *mātrāḥ,* the pitch; *balam,* the power of the voice; *sāmaḥ,* cadence; *santānaḥ,* consistency of pronunciation; *iti śīkṣādhyāyaḥ uktaḥ,* all this is explained in the chapter called Śīkṣā. *Iti dvitīyaḥ anuvākaḥ,* here ends the second chapter.

1. [Now] we will explain [what is called] pronunciation. [It consists of:] the way the various letters are pronounced, the modulations of the voice, the pitch that is maintained as you speak, the power of the voice, the cadences, and the consistency of the voice. This is what the chapter on pronunciation explains.

It is true that the purpose of reading the Upaniṣad is to get at its meaning, but you may miss that meaning if you do not know the pronunciation of each of its words. This is why the Upaniṣad tells you here what the important components of correct pronunciation are. The subject of pronunciation belongs to the branch of learning called *saṁhitā* (collection). Here it is treated as part and parcel of the Upaniṣad because of the important role it plays in the study of the Upaniṣad.

Chapter Three

सह नौ यशः। सह नौ ब्रह्मवर्चसम्। अथातः संहि-
ताया उपनिषदं व्याख्यास्यामः। पञ्चस्वधिकरणेषु। अधि-
लोकमधिज्यौतिषमधिविद्यमधिप्रजमध्यात्मम्। ता महा-
सꣳहिता इत्याचक्षते। अथाधिलोकम्। पृथिवी पूर्वरूपम्।
द्यौरुत्तररूपम्। आकाशः सन्धिः॥ १॥

वायुः सन्धानम्। इत्यधिलोकम्। अथाधिज्यौतिषम्। अग्निः पूर्वरूपम्। आदित्य उत्तररूपम्। आपः सन्धिः। वैद्युतः सन्धानम्। इत्यधिज्यौतिषम्। अथाधिविद्यम्। आचार्यः पूर्वरूपम्॥ २ ॥

अन्तेवास्युत्तरंरूपम्। विद्या सन्धिः। प्रवचनꣳ सन्धानम्। इत्यधिविद्यम्। अथाधिप्रजम्। माता पूर्वरूपम्। पितोत्तररूपम्। प्रजा सन्धिः। प्रजननꣳ सन्धानम्। इत्यधिप्रजम्॥ ३ ॥

अथाध्यात्मम्। अधरा हनुः पूर्वरूपम्। उत्तरा हनुरुत्तररूपम्। वाक्सन्धिः। जिह्वा सन्धानम्। इत्यध्यात्मम्। इतीमा महासꣳहिताः। य एवमेता महासꣳहिता व्याख्याता वेद। संधीयते प्रजया पशुभिः। ब्रह्मवर्चसेनान्नाद्येन सुवर्ग्येण लोकेन॥ ४॥ इति तृतीयोऽनुवाकः॥

Saha nau yaśaḥ; Saha nau brahmavarcasam; Athātaḥ saṁhitāyā upaniṣadaṁ vyākhyāsyāmaḥ; Pañcasvadhikaraṇeṣu; Adhilokamadhijyautiṣamadhividyamadhiprajamadhyātmam; Tā mahāsaṁhitā ityācakṣate; Athādhilokam; Pṛthivī pūrvarūpam; Dyauruttararūpam; Ākāśaḥ sandhiḥ.

Vāyuḥ sandhānam; Ityadhilokam; Athādhijyautiṣam; Agniḥ pūrvarūpam; Āditya uttararūpam; Āpaḥ sandhiḥ; Vaidyutaḥ sandhānam; Ityadhijyautiṣam; Athādhividyam; Ācāryaḥ pūrvarūpam.

Antevāsyuttararūpam; Vidyā sandhiḥ; Pravacanaṁ sandhānam; Ityadhividyam; Athādhiprajam; Mātā pūrvarūpam; Pitottararūpam; Prajā sandhiḥ; Prajananaṁ sandhānam; Ityadhiprajam.

Athādhyātmam; Adharā hanuḥ pūrvarūpam; Uttarā hanuruttararūpam; Vāksandhiḥ; Jihvā sandhānam; Ityadhyātmam; Itīmā mahāsaṁhitāḥ; Ya evametā mahāsaṁhitā vyākhyātā veda; Saṁdhīyate prajayā paśubhiḥ; Brahmavarcasenānnādyena suvargyeṇa lokena. Iti tṛtīyo-'nuvākaḥ.

Nau, both of us [the teacher and the student]; *saha,* equally; *yaśaḥ,* fame [may grow]; *nau saha brahmavarcasam,* may we both attain equally the glory that characterizes Brahman; *ataḥ,* for this reason; *atha,* henceforth; *adhilokam,* all that relates to the earth and other worlds; *adhijyautiṣam,* all that relates to fire and the things that shine; *adhividyam,* all that relates to the teacher and learning; *adhiprajam,* matters relating to the parents and the child; *adhyātmam,* things concerning the body and the mind; *pañcasu adhikaraṇeṣu,* matters relating to these five areas; *saṁhitāyāḥ,* all these allied things [constitute a kind of]; *upaniṣadam,* Upaniṣad [and the philosophy underlying them]; *vyākhyāsyāmaḥ,* we will explain; *tāḥ mahāsaṁhitāḥ iti ācakṣate,* they are all known as the Great Saṁhitā [because they deal with things of great importance]; *atha,* now; *adhilokam,* the philosophy concerning the various worlds [is being explained]; *pṛthivī pūrvarūpam,* [meditate on] the first part [of this adhiloka saṁhitā] as the earth; *dyauḥ uttararūpam,* the last part as heaven; *ākāśaḥ sandhiḥ,* the sky as the meeting point between the two.

Vāyuḥ sandhānam, air joins them; *iti adhilokam,* this is the philosophical view about the worlds; *atha adhijyautiṣam,* next, the philosophy about the luminous bodies; *agniḥ pūrvarūpam,* consider the first part as fire [and meditate accordingly]; *āditya uttararūpam,* treat the last part as Āditya, the sun; *āpaḥ sandhiḥ,* water is the meeting point; *vaidyutaḥ sandhānam,* the essence of lightning joins them; *iti adhijyautiṣam,* this is the philosophy about luminous bodies; *atha adhividyam,* next, how you meditate on learning; *ācāryaḥ pūrvarūpam,* the first part stands for the teacher.

Antevāsī uttararūpam, the resident student is the last part; *vidyā sandhiḥ,* learning is the meeting point; *pravacanam sandhānam,* joint recitation by the teacher and the student joins them; *iti adhividyam,* this is the philosophy of learning; *atha adhiprajam,* now, about progeny; *mātā pūrvarūpam,* the mother is the first part; *pitā uttararūpam,* the father is the last part; *prajā sandhiḥ,* the children represent the meeting point; *prajananam sandhānam,* procreation joins them; *iti adhiprajam,* this is the philosophy of progeny.

Atha adhyātmam, now, about the body and the mind; *adharā hanuḥ pūrvarūpam,* the lower jaw is the first part; *uttarā hanuḥ uttararūpam,* the upper jaw is the last part; *vāk sandhiḥ,* the organ of speech is the meeting point; *jihvā sandhānam,* the tongue [from the tip to the root] joins them; *iti adhyātmam,* this is the philosophy regarding the body and the mind; *iti imāḥ mahāsaṁhitāḥ.* all this together constitutes what is called the Mahāsaṁhitā; *yaḥ evam etāḥ mahāsaṁhitāḥ vyākhyātāḥ veda,* he who knows this Mahāsaṁhitā knows as explained [above]; *prajayā paśubhiḥ brahmavarcasena annādyena suvargyeṇa lokena saṁdhīyate,* he comes to possess children, animals, the brightness of Brahman, food, and heaven [i.e., he gets everything in this world or elsewhere]. *Iti tṛtīyaḥ anuvākaḥ,* here ends the third chapter.

1-4. May our fame grow equally, both the teacher's for his teaching and the student's for his capacity to learn. May we both shine with the radiance of Brahman.

[Scholarship may give you a clear insight into things, but it may not give you the knowledge of the Ultimate Reality.] This is why it is necessary that we explain the philosophy underlying the five areas—namely, those concerning the earth and other celestial bodies, those concerning fire and other luminous bodies, those concerning the teacher and other elements in the area of education, those concerning a mother and other factors concerning progeny, and those concerning the human body. These subjects together constitute a great Upaniṣad. It is called 'great' because of its importance.

We begin by explaining the Upaniṣad concerning he earth and other worlds. In this Saṁhitā, the first part is the earth, the last part is heaven, and in between is the sky. What unites them is air. If you want to meditate on these worlds, do so in this order.

Next is the meditation on fire and other luminous things. In this Saṁhitā, the first part is fire, the last part is Āditya, the sun, and in between is water. What unites them is the essence of lightning. This is how you meditate on luminous bodies.

Next is the meditation on learning. In this Saṁhitā, the first part is the teacher, the last part is the resident student, and in between is learning. What unites them is the joint recitation by the teacher and the student. This is how you meditate on learning.

Next is the meditation on progeny. In this Saṁhitā, the first part is the mother, the last is the father, and in between is the child. What unites them is procreation. This is the meditation on progeny.

Next is the meditation on the body and the mind. In this Saṁhitā, the first part is the lower jaw, the last is the upper jaw, and in between is the organ of speech. What unites them is the tongue. This is the meditation on the body and the mind.

All these together constitute the Mahāsaṁhitā, the great literature. He who knows this Mahāsaṁhitā knows what has just been explained, and he comes to possess children, animals, the radiance of Brahman, food, and heaven.

The word *atha* means here 'after.' But after what? After your extensive book reading. Book reading and scholarship may be good, but they are not enough, so the Upaniṣad advises you to meditate on the world and four other things with which you are closely connected. How you are to do this is explained in the Mahāsaṁhitā. This Mahāsaṁhitā is considered so important that it is included in the Upaniṣad.

How are you to meditate? You do not meditate on the physical aspects of these things. You meditate on the deities they represent. For instance, some people worship a round piece of stone (a *śālagrāma*) as Lord Viṣṇu, and as they do so, they meditate on Lord Viṣṇu and not on the stone. Similarly, while you meditate on these physical entities, such as the earth and other worlds, or the luminous bodies, you must remember the deities behind them and fix your mind on those deities. Through these physical forms you try to reach out to the spiritual powers they represent. But these spiritual powers all belong to Brahman. So as you meditate, you slowly realize that you are one with Brahman. This meditation is a means to progress towards Brahman. This is the message of the Saṁhitā here.

Chapter Four

यश्छन्दसामृषभो विश्वरूपः। छन्दोभ्योऽध्यमृतात्संबभूव। स मेन्द्रो मेधया स्पृणोतु। अमृतस्य देव धारणो भूयासम्। शरीरं मे विचर्षणम्। जिह्वा मे मधुमत्तमा। कर्णाभ्यां भूरि विश्रुवम्। ब्रह्मणः कोशोऽसि मेधया पिहितः। श्रुतं मे गोपाय। आवहन्ती वितन्वाना॥ १॥

कुर्वाणाऽचीरमात्मनः। वासा सिꣳमम गावश्च। अन्नपाने च सर्वदा। ततो मे श्रियमावह। लोमशां पशुभिः सह स्वाहा। आमायन्तु ब्रह्मचारिणः स्वाहा। विमाऽऽयन्तु ब्रह्मचारिणः स्वाहा। प्रमाऽऽयन्तु ब्रह्मचारिणः स्वाहा। दमायन्तु ब्रह्मचारिणः स्वाहा। शमायन्तु ब्रह्मचारिणः स्वाहा॥ २॥

Yaśchandasāmṛṣabho viśvarūpaḥ; Chandobhyo'-dhyamṛtātsaṁbabhūva; Sa mendro medhayā spṛṇotu; Amṛtasya deva dhārano bhūyāsam; Śarīraṁ me vicarṣaṇam; Jihvā me madhumattamā; Karṇābhyāṁ bhūri viśruvam; Brahmaṇaḥ kośo'si medhayā pihitaḥ; Śrutaṁ me gopāya; Āvahantī vitanvānā.

Kurvāṇā'cīramātmanaḥ; Vāsāṁsi mama gāvaśca; Annapāne ca sarvadā; Tato me śriyamāvaha; Lomaśāṁ paśubhiḥ saha svāhā; Āmāyantu brahmacāriṇaḥ svāhā; Vimā''yantu brahmacāriṇaḥ svāhā; Pramā''yantu brahmacāriṇaḥ svāhā; Damāyantu brahmacāriṇaḥ svāhā; Śamāyantu brahmacāriṇaḥ svāhā.

Yaḥ chandasām, that [i.e., Om] among the Vedic hymns; *ṛṣabhaḥ,* [is] the best [literally, a bull]; *viśvarūpaḥ,* present everywhere [in every form of speech]; *chandobhyaḥ amṛtāt,* from among the ways of attaining knowledge, i.e., from the Vedas; *adhi-saṁbabhūva,* emerged; *saḥ,* that [Om]; *indraḥ,* the God of the gods [who can give you whatever you want]; *medhayā mā spṛṇotu,* may make me intellectually strong; *deva,* O Lord; *amṛtasya dhāraṇaḥ bhūyāsam,* may I attain immortality; *me śarīram vicarṣaṇam,* may my body be fit to attain Self-knowledge; *me jihvā madhumattamā,* may I have a sweet tongue; *karṇābhyām bhūri viśruvam,* may my ears greatly help me to hear about Self-knowledge; [O Om] *medhayā,* by mundane perceptions; *pihitaḥ,* veiled; *brahmaṇaḥ kośaḥ asi,* you are the symbol of Brahman; *me śrutam gopāya,* please protect whatever I have learnt; *ātmanaḥ mama,* please let me have; *cīram vāsāṁsi,* plenty of clothes; *gāvaḥ,* cattle; *ca anna-pāne ca,* food and drink; *sarvadā,* always; *āvahantī,* bring me; *vitanvānā,* of many kinds and always multiplying; *kurvāṇā,* let the affluence be of this kind; *lomaśām,* goats and sheep with long hair; *paśubhiḥ,* other animals; *saha,* with; *śriyam,* affluence; *tataḥ,* after [I have developed a good intellect]; *me āvaha,* bring to me; *svāhā,* svāhā [the word you utter when you conclude an oblation]; *ā mā āyantu brahmacāriṇaḥ svāhā,* may students come to me from all quarters; *vi mā āyantu brahmacāriṇaḥ svāhā,* may students come to me in whatever way possible; *pra mā āyantu brahmacāriṇaḥ svāhā,* may students come to me in the way they should; *damāyantu brahmacāriṇaḥ svāhā,* may students come to me after they have fully acquired self-control so far as the body is concerned; *śamāyantu brahmacāriṇaḥ svāhā,* may students come to me after they have fully acquired self-control so far as the mind is concerned.

1-2. Om is the sum and substance of the Vedas and is present in every form of speech. The Vedas show the way to Self-realization, and Om has emerged from those Vedas. It is also identified with the God of the gods, Indra, who can give us whatever we want. I pray that Om may give me a good intellect. I also pray to the Lord [Om] that I may attain immortality. May I have a fit body to attain Self-knowledge. May I have a sweet tongue, and may my ears also help me greatly in my attempt to attain Self-knowledge. You are the symbol of Brahman, but our sense organs conceal this fact from us. Please protect the knowledge I have acquired.

[Om,] please grant me affluence. Grant me plenty of clothes, cattle, food, and drink. And grant that these may be of various kinds and that they may also keep multiplying. May my affluence also include goats and sheep with long hair, and other animals. May I have this affluence only after I have acquired a good intellect. *Svāhā.*

May students come to me from all quarters. *Svāhā.* May students come to me in whatever way possible. *Svāhā.* May students come to me in the manner they should. *Svāhā.* May students come to me after they have fully acquired control over the body. *Svāhā.* May students come to me after they have fully acquired control over the mind. *Svāhā.*

Of all the Vedic hymns, simply the word Om is the best. It is the common sound in all words, and in this sense, it is like a stick that pierces through a stack of leaves. Here it is said to be as powerful as a bull (*ṛṣabha*). It is the symbol of Indra and also Brahman. Those who want a good intellect are advised to repeat these hymns, which will also give them affluence (*śrī*).

First you ask for a good intellect, because if you don't have a good intellect, you will waste whatever good things you acquire. With the judgement that a good intellect provides, the wealth that you possess will be safe. Pray to Om for what you want. How to pray and what to pray for are given here. The Upaniṣad gives the prayer in the form of a *homa* (sacrifice). This is why the word *svāhā* is used. *Svāhā* is uttered just as the oblation is being offered into the fire.

यशो जनेऽसानि स्वाहा। श्रेयान् वस्यसोऽसानि स्वाहा। तं त्वा भग प्रविशानि स्वाहा। स मा भग प्रविश स्वाहा। तस्मिन् सहस्रशाखे निभगाहं त्वयि मृजे स्वाहा। यथाऽऽपः प्रवता यन्ति यथा मासा अहर्जरम्। एवं मां ब्रह्मचारिणः। धातरायन्तु सर्वतः स्वाहा। प्रतिवेशोऽसि प्र मा भाहि प्र मा पद्यस्व॥ ३॥ इति चतुर्थोऽनुवाकः॥

Yaśo jane'sāni svāhā; Śreyān vasyaso'sāni svāhā; Taṁ tvā bhaga praviśāni svāhā; Sa mā bhaga praviśa svāhā; Tasmin sahasraśākhe nibhagāhaṁ tvayi mṛje svāhā; Yathā''paḥ pravatā yanti yathā māsā aharjaram; Evaṁ māṁ brahmacāriṇaḥ; Dhātarāyantu sarvataḥ svāhā; Prativeśo'si pra mā bhāhi pra mā padyasva. Iti caturtho'nuvākaḥ.

Jane, in society; *yaśaḥ asāni,* may I be famous; *śreyān vasyasaḥ asāni,* may I be the foremost among the rich; *bhaga* [i.e., *bhagavān*], O Lord; *tam tvā,* into you [the symbol of Brahman]; *praviśāni,* may I enter; *bhaga,* O Lord; *saḥ,* that [i.e., you, the symbol of Brahman]; *mā,* into me; *praviśa,* enter [i.e., be one with me]; *tasmin sahasraśākhe,* in that which has many forms; *tvayi,* in you; *aham ni-mṛje,* [thereby] I completely wash off all my sins; *āpaḥ yathā pravatā yanti,* just as water flows downwards; *yathā māsāḥ aharjaram,* just as months run into years; *evam,* in the same way; *mām brahmacāriṇaḥ āyantu sarvataḥ,* let students come to me from everywhere; *dhātaḥ,* O Lord; *prativeśaḥ asi,* you are the refuge [of all]; *mā prabhāhi,* please reveal yourself to me; *mā prapadyasva,* please be one with me; [I surrender myself to you]. *Iti caturthaḥ anuvākaḥ,* here ends the fourth chapter.

3. May I be well known in society. *Svāhā.* May I be the foremost among the rich. *Svāhā.* You are the symbol of Brahman. May I merge into you. *Svāhā.* May you also merge into me. *Svāhā.* O Lord, you have many forms. May I wash off all my sins in you. *Svāhā.* Just as water runs downwards and months become years, in the same way, O Lord, may students come to me from all quarters. *Svāhā.* You give shelter to all who need it. I surrender to you. Please reveal yourself to me and be one with me.

Though the prayer here is that you may be famous and rich, you also pray that you may be one with

Brahman. Not only that, you pray that Brahman may be one with you. You may have many shortcomings, but they will all disappear when you lose yourself in Brahman. Water always goes downwards, and months always pass into years. This happens in their natural course. In the same way, you want students to rush to you from all quarters. You finally pray that you and Brahman may be totally one.

Why do you need money? You need it to perform your duties. But why do you have to perform your duties? So that all your accumulated sins may be washed away. When you have a pure mind, knowledge automatically reveals itself to you. Śaṅkara quotes a verse which says: 'If the surface of the mirror is clean, you can then have a clear view of yourself.' So also, to attain Self-knowledge you have to have a pure, clean mind. This is the purpose of this prayer.

Chapter Five

भूर्भुवः सुवरिति वा एतास्तिस्रो व्याहृतयः। तासामु ह स्मैतां चतुर्थीम्। माहाचमस्यः प्रवेदयते। मह इति। तद्ब्रह्म। स आत्मा। अङ्गान्यन्या देवताः। भूरिति वा अयं लोकः। भुव इत्यन्तरिक्षम्। सुवरित्यसौ लोकः॥ १॥

मह इत्यादित्यः। आदित्येन वाव सर्वे लोका महीयन्ते। भूरिति वा अग्निः। भुव इति वायुः। सुवरित्यादित्यः।

मह इति चन्द्रमाः। चन्द्रमसा वाव सर्वाणि ज्योतीꣳषि महीयन्ते। भूरिति वा ऋचः। भुव इति सामानि। सुवरिति यजूꣳसि॥ २॥

मह इति ब्रह्म। ब्रह्मणा वाव सर्वे वेदा महीयन्ते। भूरिति वै प्राणः। भुव इत्यपानः। सुवरिति व्यानः। मह इत्यन्नम्। अन्नेन वाव सर्वे प्राणा महीयन्ते। ता वा एताश्चतस्रश्चतुर्धा। चतस्रश्चतस्रो व्याहृतयः। ता यो वेद। स वेद ब्रह्म। सर्वेऽस्मै देवा बलिमावहन्ति॥ ३॥ इति पञ्चमोऽनुवाकः॥

Bhūrbhuvaḥ suvariti vā etāstisro vyāhṛtayaḥ; Tāsāmu ha smaitāṁ caturthīm; Māhācamasyaḥ pravedayate; Maha iti; Tadbrahma; Sa ātmā; Aṅgānyanyā devatāḥ; Bhūriti vā ayaṁ lokaḥ; Bhuva ityantarikṣam; Suvaritya-sau lokaḥ.

Maha ityādityaḥ; Ādityena vāva sarve lokā mahīyante; Bhūriti vā agniḥ; Bhuva iti vāyuḥ; Suvarityādityaḥ; Maha iti candramāḥ; Candramasā vāva sarvāṇi jyotīṁṣi mahīyante; Bhūriti vā ṛcaḥ; Bhuva iti sāmāni; Suvariti yajūṁsi.

Maha iti brahma; Brahmaṇā vāva sarve vedā mahīyante; Bhūriti vai prāṇaḥ; Bhuva ityapānaḥ; Suvariti vyānaḥ; Maha ityannam; Annena vāva sàrve prāṇā mahīyante; Tā vā etāścatasraścaturdhā; Catasraścatasro vyāhṛtayaḥ; Tā yo veda; Sa veda brahma; Sarve'smai devā balimāvahanti. Iti pañcamo'nuvākaḥ.

Bhūḥ, the earth; *bhuvaḥ,* the space between the earth and heaven; *suvaḥ,* heaven; *iti,* thus; *etāḥ,* these; *tisraḥ,* three [so-called]; *vyāhṛtayaḥ,* vyāhṛtis [mystical utterances, supposedly capable of removing all difficulties]; *tāsām u ha caturthīm,* these are followed by a fourth; *mahaḥ iti,* [called] maha; *māhācamasyaḥ,* Māhācamasya, the son of the sage Mahācamasa; *pravedayate sma etām,* discovered it; *tat,* that [the self-luminous maha]; *brahma,* is Brahman [beyond time and space]; *saḥ ātmā,* he is the Self; *anyāḥ,* the others [that is, bhūḥ, bhuvaḥ, and suvaḥ]; *devatāḥ,* the deities [presiding over them]; *aṅgāni,* are their part and parcel; *bhūḥ iti vai ayam lokaḥ,* bhūḥ is this earth; *bhuvaḥ iti antarikṣam,* bhuvaḥ is the space between the earth and heaven; *asau lokaḥ suvaḥ iti,* that space over there is heaven, suvaḥ.

Ādityaḥ mahaḥ iti, Āditya [the sun] is maha; *ādityena vāva sarve lokāḥ mahīyante,* for if all the planets grow [or, are able to function as they do] it is because of Āditya; *bhūḥ iti vai agniḥ,* fire is bhūḥ; *bhuvaḥ iti vāyuḥ,* air is bhuvaḥ; *suvaḥ iti ādityaḥ,* Āditya [the sun] is suvaḥ; *mahaḥ iti candramāḥ,* Candra [the moon] is maha; *candramasā vāva sarvāṇi jyotīṁṣi mahīyante,* all luminous bodies grow [or, are able to function the way they do] because of the moon; *bhūḥ iti vai ṛcaḥ,* the Ṛg Veda is bhūḥ; *bhuvaḥ iti sāmāni,* the Sāma Veda is bhuvaḥ; *suvaḥ iti yajūṁsi,* the Yajur Veda is suvaḥ.

Mahaḥ iti brahma, maha is Brahman [Om]; *brahmaṇā vāva,* because of Brahman; *sarve vedāḥ mahīyante,* all the Vedas gain in strength; *bhūḥ iti vai prāṇaḥ,* bhūḥ is prāṇa [the air we breathe in]; *bhuvaḥ iti apānaḥ,* bhuvaḥ is apāna [the air we breathe out]; *suvaḥ iti vyānaḥ,* suvaḥ is vyāna [the air that goes all over the body]; *mahaḥ iti annam,* maha is food; *annena vāva sarve prāṇāḥ mahīyante,* for food gives strength to all the prāṇas [i.e., to all the aspects of the vital breath]; *tāḥ vai etāḥ catasraḥ,* all these four; *vyāhṛtayaḥ,* vyāhṛtis [utterances]; *catasraḥ catasraḥ caturdhā,* are described under four categories; *tāḥ yaḥ veda,* he who knows these [four vyāhṛtis]; *saḥ veda brahma,* he knows Brahman; *sarve asmai devāḥ,* to him all the gods; *balim āvahanti,* bring offerings. *Iti pañcamaḥ anuvākaḥ,* here ends the fifth chapter.

1-3. Bhūḥ, bhuvaḥ, and suvaḥ—these three are the well-known mystical utterances [vyāhṛtis]. Following these three, a fourth—maha—was discovered by the sage Māhācamasya, son of the sage Mahācamasa. Maha is no other than Brahman, the Self. Bhūḥ, bhuvaḥ, and suvaḥ, and their presiding deities, are all part and parcel of Brahman. Bhūḥ is the earth, bhuvaḥ is the space between the earth and heaven, and suvaḥ [or, svaḥ] is heaven. Maha is Āditya, the source of cosmic life. This Āditya gives strength to the other worlds.

Bhūḥ is Agni [fire], bhuvaḥ is Vāyu [air], and suvaḥ is Āditya [the sun]. Maha is Candra [the moon], for all luminous bodies get their light from the moon. Bhūḥ is known as the Ṛg Veda, bhuvaḥ the Sāma Veda, and suvaḥ the Yajur Veda. Maha is Brahman [Om], because from Brahman the Vedas get their strength.

Bhūḥ is prāṇa [the air we breathe in], bhuvaḥ is apāna [the air we breathe out], and suvaḥ is vyāna [the air that is all over the body]. Maha is food, because food gives strength to all functions of the vital breath. There are four vyāhṛtis [utterances], and each of them can assume four forms. If you know the real significance of these four utterances, you then know Brahman and all the deities will bring you their gifts.

Previously (in chapter three) the saṁhitā was explained, for it is necessary to understand its significance. The saṁhitā has to be used for purposes of meditation. Next, those who want a good intellect and then affluence have been advised what mantras they should repeat.

Now you are being told how, in order to attain Self-knowledge, you should meditate on bhūḥ, bhuvaḥ, suvaḥ, etc. And you are especially reminded of the importance of maha. The Upaniṣad says that the sage Māhācamasya realized that maha and Brahman were one and the same, and that the three—bhūḥ, bhuvaḥ, suvaḥ—were all part of that Brahman (maha). They are manifestations of Brahman and should be thought of as such. In short, you are told that if you understand the vyāhṛtis, you will have no difficulty in realizing Brahman. Apparently they stand for minor deities, but taken together they are Brahman.

Chapter Six

स य एषोऽन्तर्हृदय आकाशः। तस्मिन्नयं पुरुषो मनोमयः। अमृतो हिरण्मयः। अन्तरेण तालुके। य एष स्तन इवावलम्बते। सेन्द्रयोनिः। यत्रासौ केशान्तो विवर्तते। व्यपोह्य शीर्षकपाले। भूरित्यग्नौ प्रतितिष्ठति। भुव इति वायौ॥ १॥

सुवरित्यादित्ये। मह इति ब्रह्मणि। आप्नोति स्वाराज्यम्। आप्नोति मनसस्पतिम्। वाक्पतिश्चक्षुष्पतिः। श्रोत्रपतिर्विज्ञानपतिः। एतत्ततो भवति। आकाशशरीरं ब्रह्म। सत्यात्म प्राणारामं मन आनन्दम्। शान्तिसमृद्धममृतम्। इति प्राचीनयोग्योपास्स्व॥ २॥ इति षष्ठोऽनुवाकः॥

Sa ya eṣo'ntarhṛdaya ākāśaḥ; Tasminnayaṁ puruṣo manomayaḥ; Amṛto hiraṇmayaḥ; Antareṇa tāluke; Ya eṣa stana ivāvalambate; Sendrayoniḥ; Yatrāsau keśānto vivartate; Vyapohya śīrṣakapāle; Bhūrityagnau pratitiṣṭhati; Bhuva iti vāyau.

Suvarityāditye; Maha iti brahmaṇi; Āpnoti svārājyam; Āpnoti manasaspatim; Vākpatiścakṣuṣpatiḥ; Śrotrapatirvijñānapatiḥ; Etattato bhavati; Ākāśaśarīraṁ brahma; Satyātma prāṇārāmaṁ mana ānandam; Śāntisamṛddhamamṛtam; Iti prācīnayogyopāssva. Iti ṣaṣṭho'nuvākaḥ.

Antaḥ hṛdaye, inside the heart; *yaḥ eṣaḥ ākāṣaḥ,* the empty space which is there; *tasmin,* in that [space]; *saḥ ayam,* there is this; *manomayaḥ,* [representing] the Cosmic Mind; *amṛtaḥ,* immortal; *hiraṇmayaḥ,* luminous; *puruṣaḥ,* self [exists]; *antareṇa tāluke,* between the two palates; *yaḥ eṣaḥ,* that [piece of flesh] which; *stana iva,* like a nipple; *avalambate,* is hanging; *yatra,* where; *asau keśāntaḥ,* the roots of the hairs; *vivartate,* divide; [the suṣumnā vein] *vyapohya,* pierces through; *śīrṣakapāle,* the two palates of the head; *sā,* this [vein, the suṣumnā, is]; *indrayoniḥ,* where Indra [i.e., Brahman] manifests itself; [going out along this suṣumnā, the puruṣa, or self] *bhūḥ iti agnau pratitiṣṭhati,* merges into Agni [fire], which is bhūḥ; *bhuvaḥ iti vāyau,* [and also] into Vāyu [air], which is bhuvaḥ.

Suvaḥ iti āditye, into Āditya [the sun], which is suvaḥ; *maha iti brahmaṇi,* into Brahman, which is maha; *svārājyam āpnoti,* he realizes his identity with Brahman; *manasaspatim āpnoti,* he realizes his identity with that [Brahman] which controls the mind and all its activities; *vākpatiḥ cakṣuspatih śrotrapatiḥ vijñānapatiḥ,* which controls the speech, the eyes, the ears,. and the mind [i.e., all the organs]; *tataḥ etat bhavati,* following this, he becomes; *ākāśaśarīram,* with a body like all-pervasive space; *brahma,* [he becomes] Brahman; *satyātma,* he becomes truth itself; *prāṇārāmam,* he is happy with himself; *manaḥ ānandam,* his mind is full of bliss; *śāntisamṛddham,* the embodiment of peace; *amṛtam,* immortality; *prācīnayogya,* O Prācīnayogya [O timeless one]; *upāssva,* worship [that Brahman]. *Iti ṣaṣṭhaḥ anuvākaḥ,* here ends the sixth chapter.

1-2. There is an empty space in the heart, and in that is the immortal and luminous Self, representing the Cosmic Mind. Between the two palates there is hanging a piece of flesh which looks like a nipple. Here the roots of the hair divide. Through here also [runs a vein called the *suṣumnā*] which pierces between the two sides of the skull. This vein is Indrayoni, where Indra [i.e., Brahman] manifests itself. The individual who realizes the Self goes out along this suṣumnā, and then merges with Agni [fire] and becomes one with bhūḥ. Then he merges into Vāyu [air] and becomes one with bhuvaḥ. Then he merges into Āditya [the sun] and becomes one with suvaḥ. And finally he merges into Brahman which is maha. He then realizes his identity with Brahman and attains full control over his mind. As the lord of the mind, he realizes that he is also the lord of all the organs—of speech, the eyes, the ears, and also consciousness. He is all-pervasive like the sky. He is Truth itself, and he is content in the Self. His mind is full of bliss. He becomes that Brahman, which is the embodiment of peace and happiness and is also immortal. O Prācīnayogya, worship that Brahman.

The heart is like a lotus, and inside this lotus there is an empty space where the Self lies. The Self is described here as the *puruṣa* because it 'fills' (*pūrṇa*) everything, and also because it 'lies' (*śayana*) in the heart, which is its abode (*pura*). The Self is also described as *manomaya* because it is the sum total of all minds, and also because it is consciousness itself. This Self is immortal and it is also luminous.

But how do you realize this Self? The yoga scriptures say that there is a vein called the *suṣumnā* which goes upward from the heart into the head. It runs between the palates and pierces through the head. This passage is called here *indrayoni. Indra* means Brahman, and *indrayoni* means the place where Brahman is manifest. It is here that you realize that you are Brahman, the Cosmic Self. When you realize this, you leave the body and merge into the phenomenal world—into Agni (fire), which is bhūḥ; into Vāyu (air), which is bhuvaḥ; into Āditya (the sun), which is suvaḥ; and then into Brahman, which is the fourth vyāhṛti, maha. That is to say, first you merge into Agni and other deities. Ultimately, however, all these vyāhṛtis and their presiding deities merge into Brahman.

Brahman is supreme, so when you realize that you are Brahman you also realize that you are the Lord of everything, including your organs and mind. You are then vast, infinite. You are all-pervasive like space and free from all limitations. You are Truth itself. You are bliss itself. You are full. This is what happens when you realize you are Brahman.

Always meditate that you are Brahman.

Chapter Seven

पृथिव्यन्तरिक्षं द्यौर्दिशोऽवान्तरदिशाः। अग्निर्वायु-
रादित्यश्चन्द्रमा नक्षत्राणि। आप ओषधयो वनस्पतय
आकाश आत्मा। इत्यधिभूतम्। अथाध्यात्मम्। प्राणो
व्यानोऽपान उदानः समानः। चक्षुः श्रोत्रं मनो वाक्
त्वक्। चर्म माꣳसꣳ स्नावास्थि मज्जा। एतदधिविधाय
ऋषिरवोचत्। पाङ्क्तं वा इदꣳ सर्वम्। पाङ्क्तेनैव
पाङ्क्तꣳ स्पृणोतीति॥ १॥ इति सप्तमोऽनुवाकः॥

Pṛthivyantarikṣaṁ dyaurdiśo'vāntaradiśāḥ; Agnir-vāyurādityaścandramā nakṣatrāṇi; Āpa oṣadhayo vanas-pataya ākāśa ātmā; Ityadhibhūtam; Athādhyātmam; Prāṇo vyāno'pāna udānaḥ samānaḥ; Cakṣuḥ śrotraṁ mano vāk tvak; Carma māṁsaṁ snāvāsthi majjā; Etadadhividhāya ṛṣiravocat; Pāṅktaṁ vā idaṁ sarvam; Pāṅktenaiva pāṅktaṁ spṛṇotīti. Iti saptamo'nuvākaḥ.

Pṛthivī, the earth; *antarikṣam,* the mid-region; *dyauḥ,* heaven; *diśaḥ,* the quarters [east, west, etc.]; *avāntara-diśāḥ,* the intermediate quarters [like the vyāhṛtis earlier mentioned, the four-fold divinities]; *agniḥ,* fire; *vāyuḥ,* air; *ādityaḥ,* the sun; *candramāḥ,* the moon; *nakṣatrāṇi,* the stars; *āpaḥ,* water; *oṣadhayaḥ,* herbs; *vanaspatayaḥ,* trees [bearing fruits without flowers]; *ākāśaḥ,* space; *ātmā,* the body; *iti adhibhūtam,* these are the five-fold elements; *atha adhyātmam,* now, coming to the body;

prāṇaḥ, the air that is inhaled; *vyānaḥ,* the air that spreads throughout the body; *apānaḥ,* the air you breathe out; *udānaḥ,* the air that pushes things upwards; *samānaḥ,* the air that distributes blood and other fluids all over the body; *cakṣuḥ,* the eyes; *śrotram,* the ears; *manaḥ,* the mind; *vāk,* the organ of speech; *tvak,* the organ of touch; *carma,* skin; *māṁsam,* muscle; *snāvā,* nerves [or veins]; *asthi,* bone; *majjā,* marrow; *ṛṣiḥ,* a sage [well-versed in the Vedas]; *etat,* this [division of things in fives]; *adhividhāya,* having conceived; *avocat,* he preached; *pāṅktam vai idam sarvam,* all this is fivefold; *pāṅktena eva pāṅktam spṛṇoti iti,* by such meditation the external fivefold becomes one with the internal fivefold. *Iti saptamaḥ anuvākaḥ,* here ends the seventh chapter.

1. The earth [bhūḥ], the intermediate space between the earth and heaven [bhuvaḥ], heaven [suvaḥ], the four quarters [east, west, and so on], and the four subquarters [northeast, northwest, and so on]—[these five constitute the *loka pāṅkta,* the group of lokas]. Agni [fire], Vāyu [air], Āditya [the sun], Candra [the moon], and Nakṣatra [the stars]—[these five constitute the *devatā pāṅkta,* the group of devatās (shining bodies)]. Water, plants, the *vanaspati* [i.e., large trees which have fruits but no flowers], Ākāśa [space], and the body—[these five are the *bhūta pāṅkta,* the group of elements]. Here, three kinds of *pāṅktas* are mentioned. Worship of Brahman through these *pāṅktas* is called *adhibhūta* worship—worship of physical objects. Now comes *adhyātma* worship—worship of the body. Prāṇa [the air we inhale], vyāna

[the air which is between prāṇa and apāna], apāna [the air we exhale and which ejects things from the body], udāna [the air that pushes things up], and samāna [the air that reduces the digested food to blood and other fluids]—[these five are the *prāṇa pāṅkta,* the group of vital airs]. The eyes, the ears, the mind, the organ of speech, and the organ of touch—[these five are the *indriya pāṅkta,* the group of organs]. Skin, flesh, nerves, bones, and marrow —[these five are the *dhātu pāṅkta,* the group of the constituents of the body]. A sage prescribed this worship of Brahman as the *pāṅktas.* These *pāṅktas* are all fivefold. They are also interdependent. They are, in fact, one and the same.

Earlier, Brahman was conceived as the fourfold vyāhṛtis. Now, in this verse, the worship of Brahman as the *pāṅktas* is being presented. However, it is the unity of existence that is being stressed here. External or internal, fivefold or otherwise—these expressions do not matter. What matters is the oneness of things. When a person realizes this, he is the Lord of the universe, because he becomes one with Brahman.

Chapter Eight

ओमिति ब्रह्म। ओमितीद॑ सर्वम्। ओमित्येतदनुकृतिर्ह स्म वा अप्यो श्रावयेत्याश्रावयन्ति। ओमिति सामानि

गायन्ति। ओꣳशोमिति शस्त्राणि शꣳसन्ति। ओमित्यध्वर्युः प्रतिगरं प्रतिगृणाति। ओमिति ब्रह्मा प्रसौति। ओमित्यग्निहोत्रमनुजानाति। ओमिति ब्राह्मणः प्रवक्ष्यन्नाह ब्रह्मोपाप्नवानीति। ब्रह्मैवोपाप्नोति॥ १॥ इति अष्टमोऽनुवाकः॥

Omiti brahma; Omitīdaṁ sarvam; Omityetadanukṛtirha sma vā apyo śrāvayetyāśrāvayanti; Omiti sāmāni gāyanti; Oṁśomiti śastrāṇi śaṁsanti; Omityadhvaryuḥ pratigaraṁ pratigṛṇāti; Omiti brahmā prasauti; Omityagnihotramanujānāti; Omiti brāhmaṇaḥ pravakṣyannāha brahmopāpnavānīti; Brahmaivopāpnoti. Iti aṣṭamo'nuvākaḥ.

Om iti brahma, the word Om is Brahman itself; *om iti idam sarvam,* [for] Om is everything; *om iti etat anukṛtiḥ ha sma vai,* Om also indicates agreement; *api,* also; *o śrāvaya iti āśrāvayanti,* priests say 'Om' when they ask other priests to start reciting the hymns [to the gods and goddesses]; *om iti sāmāni gāyanti,* as the priests start reciting the Sāma hymns, they say 'Om'; *om śom iti,* they say, 'Om śom'; *śastrāṇi,* [non-musical] hymns from the Ṛg Veda [which are called *śastras*]; *śaṁsanti,* start singing; *adhvaryuḥ,* a priest in a Yajuḥ sacrifice; *pratigṛṇāti pratigaram om iti,* in everything he does he says 'Om'; *brahmā,* another kind of priest; *om iti prasauti,* says 'Om,' indicating approval of something; *om iti agnihotram anujānāti,* those who perform the Agnihotra sacrifice say 'Om' to signal the beginning of the sacrifice; *om iti brāhmaṇaḥ pravakṣyan āha brahma upāpnavāni iti,* a brāhmin says 'Om' when he wishes to study the Vedas in order to realize Brahman; *brahma eva upāpnoti,* he [eventually] does realize Brahman.

1. The word *Om* is Brahman, for the word represents everything. It is also used to imply assent. When you say to the priests, 'Say "Om" to the gods and goddesses,' they do so. The priests begin by saying 'Om' when they recite the Sāma hymns. [Similarly,] when they recite the śastras, they begin with 'Om śom.' The Adhvaryu priest [the priest of the Yajur Veda] keeps repeating 'Om' whenever he does anything, and the priest called Brahmā says 'Om' to indicate his approval of something. Those who perform the Agnihotra sacrifice say 'Om' to signal the beginning of the sacrifice. The brāhmins as a class study the Vedas so that they may realize Brahman, but before they begin their study they say 'Om.' As a result, they realize Brahman.

Earlier the vyāhṛtis and the fivefold constituents were introduced as symbols of Brahman, and we were advised to meditate on them as such. Now Om is being introduced, not merely as a symbol of Brahman, but as Brahman itself. Om is everything just as Brahman is everything. Om is both Para Brahman (Brahman without attributes) and Apara Brahman (Brahman with attributes).

In this chapter the word *iti* follows Om. *Iti* means 'this.' It is significant, because it shows the real identity of Om—that Om is Brahman, and that it should be meditated upon that way. Om embraces all words, just as Brahman embraces all things.

The use of Om characterizes every aspect of life, spiritual and secular. If you want to realize Brahman, you begin by studying the scriptures to that end, and before you start you say 'Om.' It is Om that finally leads you to your goal, because it is Om that you are seeking, Om and Brahman being the same.

Chapter Nine

ऋतं च स्वाध्यायप्रवचने च। सत्यं च स्वाध्यायप्रवचने च। तपश्च स्वाध्यायप्रवचने च। दमश्च स्वाध्यायप्रवचने च। शमश्च स्वाध्यायप्रवचने च। अग्नयश्च स्वाध्यायप्रवचने च। अग्निहोत्रं च स्वाध्यायप्रवचने च। अतिथयश्च स्वाध्यायप्रवचने च। मानुषं च स्वाध्यायप्रवचने च। प्रजा च स्वाध्यायप्रवचने च। प्रजनश्च स्वाध्यायप्रवचने च। प्रजातिश्च स्वाध्यायप्रवचने च। सत्यमिति सत्यवचा राथीतरः। तप इति तपोनित्यः पौरुशिष्टिः। स्वाध्यायप्रवचने एवेति नाको मौद्गल्यः। तद्धि तपस्तद्धि तपः॥ १॥

इति नवमोऽनुवाकः॥

Ṛtaṁ ca svādhyāyapravacane ca; Satyaṁ ca svādhyāyapravacane ca; Tapaśca svādhyāyapravacane ca; Damaśca svādhyāyapravacane ca; Śamaśca svādhyāyapravacane ca; Agnayaśca svādhyāyapravacane ca;

Agnihotraṁ ca svādhyāyapravacane ca; Atithayaśca svādhyāyapravacane ca; Manuṣaṁ ca svādhyāyapravacane ca; Prajā ca svādhyāyapravacane ca; Prajanaśca svādhyāyapravacane ca; Prajātiśca svādhyāyapravacane ca; Satyamiti satyavacā rāthītaraḥ; Tapa iti taponityaḥ pauruśiṣṭiḥ; Svādhyāyapravacane eveti nāko maudgalyaḥ; Taddhi tapastaddhi tapaḥ. Iti navamo'nuvākaḥ.

Ṛtam, work according to the scriptures; *ca svādhyāyapravacane ca,* and also study the scriptures and teach them; *satyam,* be honest [in thought, speech, and action]; *ca svādhyāyapravacane ca,* and also study the scriptures and teach them; *tapaḥ ca svādhyāyapravacane ca,* live an austere life, and also study the scriptures and teach them; *damaḥ ca svādhyāya* [etc.], control your physical organs and also study [etc.]; *śamaḥ ca svādhyāya* [etc.], control your internal organs, and also study [etc.]; *agnayaḥ ca svādhyāya* [etc.], [kindle] the three fires [the Gārhapatya, the Āhavanīya, and the Dakṣiṇāgni], and also study [etc.]; *agnihotram ca svādhyāya* [etc.], perform the Agnihotra sacrifice, and also study [etc.]; *atithayaḥ ca svādhyāya* [etc.], show due respect to guests, and also study [etc.]; *manuṣam ca svādhyāya* [etc.], live like a normal human being, and also study [etc.]; *prajā ca svādhyāya* [etc.], have children, and also study [etc.]; *prajanaḥ ca svādhyāya* [etc.], continue the family line, and also study [etc.]; *prajātiḥ ca svādhyāya* [etc.], have grandchildren [i.e., arrange marriages for your children], and also study [etc.]; *rāthītaraḥ satyavacāḥ,* Satyavacā, of the family of Rathītara [thinks]; *satyam iti,* truth alone is enough; *pauruśiṣṭiḥ taponityaḥ,* Pauruśiṣṭi, the son of Puruśiṣṭi, known as Taponitya [thinks]; *tapaḥ iti,* the right thing is to concentrate on austerities; *nākaḥ maudgalyaḥ,* [according to] Nāka, the son of Mudgala; *svādhyāyapravacane eva iti,* [the only way] is through studying and teaching the scriptures; *tat hi tapaḥ tat hi tapaḥ,* that alone is the real austerity, that alone is the real austerity. *Iti navamaḥ anuvākaḥ,* here ends the ninth chapter.

1. Do your duties according to the scriptures, and also study the scriptures and teach them. Be honest in thought, speech, and action, and also study the scriptures and teach them. Live an austere life, and also study the scriptures and teach them. Control your physical organs, and also study the scriptures and teach them. Control your internal organs, and also study the scriptures and teach them. Maintain the three fires [used in the Agnihotra sacrifice—Gārhapatya, Āhavanīya, and Dakṣiṇāgni], and also study the scriptures and teach them. Perform the Agnihotra sacrifice every day, and also study the scriptures and teach them. Treat your guests with great respect, and also study the scriptures and teach them. Live like a normal human being, and also study the scriptures and teach them. Have children, and also study the scriptures and teach them. Continue your family line, and also study the scriptures and teach them. Arrange marriages for your children so that you have grandchildren, and also study the scriptures and teach them. Satyavacā, of the family of Rathītara, thinks that truth alone is enough. Pauruśiṣṭi, the son of Puruśiṣṭi, who is known as Taponitya thinks that one

should concentrate on austerities. But according to Nāka, the son of Mudgala, the only way is through studying and teaching the scriptures. That alone is the real austerity. That alone is the real austerity.

It has been stated earlier that only Self-knowledge can give liberation. This may lead people to think that karma (that is, the duties prescribed by the scriptures) is redundant. Lest people make this mistake, the place of karma, or duties, is being shown here. Karma properly done produces *cittaśuddhi,* a pure mind, and *cittaśuddhi* is a prerequisite for the attainment of Self-knowledge.

Everyone has to attain Self-knowledge, be he a householder or a monastic. But a householder is not yet ready to renounce everything for Self-knowledge. He first has to eat the bitter fruit of *saṁsāra,* worldly life, in order to realize its hollowness. He can then start discriminating about what is real and what is not real. This is the starting point of the mental process that ends up giving him the kind of attitude which totally rejects the world of sense pleasure and sets him in search of the Self. The process is hastened if he lives the kind of life the scriptures advise.

Some scholars think, however, that rather than performing the duties the scriptures mention, you would do well to be truthful or be austere, or to whole-heartedly study and teach the scriptures.

Chapter Ten

अहं वृक्षस्य रेरिवा। कीर्तिः पृष्ठं गिरेरिव। ऊर्ध्वपवित्रो वाजिनीव स्वमृतमस्मि। द्रविणꣳ सवर्चसम्। सुमेधा अमृतोक्षितः। इति त्रिशङ्कोर्वेदानुवचनम्॥ १॥ इति दशमोऽनुवाकः॥

Ahaṁ vṛkṣasya rerivā; Kīrtiḥ pṛṣṭhaṁ gireriva; Ūrdhvapavitro vājinīva svamṛtamasmi; Draviṇaṁ savarcasam; Sumedhā amṛtokṣitaḥ; Iti triśaṅkorvedānuvacanam. Iti daśamo'nuvākaḥ.

Aham vṛkṣasya rerivā, I am the inspirer of this tree [i.e., this world]; *gireḥ pṛṣṭham iva kīrtiḥ,* my glory is as high as the peak of a mountain; *ūrdhvapavitraḥ,* [i.e., *ūrdhvam,* origin, source; *pavitram,* pure (because it gives knowledge)], my source is Para Brahman; *vājini,* in the sun [so-called because the sun gives *vājam,* food]; *iva,* similarly; *su,* pure; *amṛtam,* liberation, or Self-knowledge; *asmi,* I have attained; *draviṇam savarcasam,* I am precious like money [I am luminous like the Self]; *sumedhāḥ,* I have a good intellect; *amṛtaḥ,* I have no fear of death; *akṣitaḥ,* I am never hurt [i.e., I am always the same]; *iti triśaṅkoḥ vedānuvacanam,* this is what the sage Triśaṅku taught after realizing the Self. *Iti daśamaḥ anuvākaḥ,* here ends the tenth chapter.

1. I am the inspirer of this tree called the world. My glory is as high as the mountain-peak. The sun gives food and thereby gives immortality to all. The sun is high [above the earth] and pure. I am also high and pure, because I am Para Brahman. [Para Brahman is always present in my consciousness.] I am precious like money, and I am luminous like the Self. I have a sharp intellect. I have no fear of death, and I am always the same. This is what the sage Triśaṅku said after realizing the Self.

This verse is in praise of the Self, and it is meant to be repeated again and again. Such repetition prepares the mind for Self-realization.

This world is rooted in the Self. The Self is pure and supreme. It is the highest. Real happiness is only in the Self and not in money, but only a pure intellect can realize the Self. It is self-luminous, beyond death, and immune to any disease or change of any sort. The sage Triśaṅku realized the Self, and this is how he described it.

Keep repeating this verse, and along with it, do your duties without any attachment to the results of your actions. This is the way you can realize the Self.

Chapter Eleven

वेदमनूच्याचार्योऽन्तेवासिनमनुशास्ति। सत्यं वद। धर्मं चर। स्वाध्यायान्मा प्रमदः। आचार्याय प्रियं धनमाहृत्य

प्रजातन्तुं मा व्यवच्छेत्सीः। सत्यान्न प्रमदितव्यम्। धर्मान्न प्रमदितव्यम्। कुशलान्न प्रमदितव्यम्। भूत्यै न प्रमदितव्यम्। स्वाध्यायप्रवचनाभ्यां न प्रमदितव्यम्॥ १॥

Vedamanūcyācāryo'ntevāsinamanuśāsti; Satyaṁ vada; Dharmaṁ cara; Svādhyāyānmā pramadaḥ; Ācāryāya priyaṁ dhanamāhṛtya prajātantuṁ mā vyavacchetsīḥ; Satyānna pramaditavyam; Dharmānna pramaditavyam; Kuśalānna pramaditavyam; Bhūtyai na pramaditavyam; Svādhyāyapravacanābhyāṁ na pramaditavyam.

Ācāryaḥ antevāsinam vedam anūcya, after teaching the student the Vedas, the teacher; *anuśāsti,* gives him [the following] instructions; *satyam vada,* tell the truth [as far as you can judge from the available evidence]; *dharmam cara,* act according to the instructions of the scriptures; *svādhyāyāt mā pramadaḥ,* never give up the habit of reading the Vedas; *ācāryāya priyam dhanam āhṛtya,* give the teacher things he likes [and then, as advised by him]; *prajātantum mā vyavacchetsīḥ,* raise a family to ensure that there is no break in your line; *satyāt na pramaditavyam,* never deviate from truth; *dharmāt na pramaditavyam,* never deviate from dharma [from performing your duties according to the scriptures]; *kuśalāt na pramaditavyam,* don't neglect taking necessary steps for self-defence; *bhūtyai na pramaditavyam,* don't be negligent where your own interests are at stake; *svādhyāyapravacanābhyām na pramaditavyam,* don't neglect reading the scriptures and teaching them to others [also, beware that you rightly and fully observe the rules enunciated above].

1. The teacher first teaches the Vedas to his disciple and then gives the following instructions: Always speak the truth according to your understanding and knowledge. Perform the duties laid down by the scriptures. Never neglect studying the scriptures. Give your teacher things he needs and likes. [When your teacher so directs, marry and raise a family.] See that there is no break in the family line. Never deviate from truth. Never neglect doing the things the scriptures prescribe. Don't neglect doing what is needed for self-defence, and don't neglect doing what is good for you. Once again, don't neglect reading the scriptures and teaching them to others. [Carry out these duties as best you can.]

In the old days in India they had what is called the *gurukula* system of education. Students from different families selected a teacher and went to live with him for a number of years while they studied with him. Living with the teacher was considered very important. It is not that the students had contact with the teacher only in the classroom. They were constantly with him. They were learning all the time. They lived as members of the teacher's family, like his own children. They shared the same food, the same comforts, and the same discomforts. There was more than just intellectual communication. They learned as they ate together, as they worked together, and as they played together. Living in such close proximity to the teacher, the students could watch what kind of life he led, how he studied, how he spent his time.

The teacher has so much knowledge that he would like to share it with the students. But then, the students must be ready to receive it. They become ready through *seva,* personal service. *Seva* implies humility and respect—respect for the teacher and for the knowledge that he has. When the teacher is pleased with the student, he gladly gives his best. In fact, he finds joy in giving whatever knowledge he has.

The tendency today is to refer to books. Perhaps we cannot help it. There is so much to know. But what do books teach? Very little. Our elders, the people around us, are all living books.

Ācārya is the teacher. Who is an ācārya? An ācārya is one who collects (*ācinoti*), or gathers, the purport of the scriptures (*śāstrārtham*). Then he practises (*ācarate*) what the scriptures say. And by this he exemplifies or illustrates it in his own life. The idea is that you must learn from a person who actually practises what he teaches. Only then does his teaching have authenticity. If a teacher only repeats what he has been told by others, then he is no better than a record player or tape recorder. People are not impressed by what he says because he does not speak with conviction, from his personal experience. But if a teacher practises what he teaches, and also has experienced what he teaches, then he can speak with authority. What is important is the teacher himself. If he is teaching the scriptures, he must be a person of God-realization. He must have realized the truth.

Then, having taught the students, the teacher gives them some final instructions (*anuśāsti*). The teacher says: 'Look, I have taught you everything. Having understood it all, now you should put it in practice. Apply your minds to whatever I have taught you. Now you must use your own judgement.'

The first instruction is *satyam vada,* speak the truth. What is the truth? Śaṅkara says that truth is what you know to be true by experience and by observation. Say only that which you yourself know to be true, about which you have had personal experience. Do not say anything on the basis of rumour or hearsay. You hear so many things. People love to gossip. But don't pass these things off as the truth.

The next instruction is *dharmam cara,* do that which is right. Here again, how do we know what is right? First of all, the scriptures tell us what is right and what is wrong. If there is any doubt, then use your own judgement. But if you still cannot decide, then follow the example of the wise, those who are superior to you. Do what they do.

Literally, *svādhyāyāt mā pramadaḥ* means never deviate from studying, from learning. The goal of life is to seek the Self, the Ultimate Truth. You must never give up this quest. You may go to teachers, and you may take the help of books, but this search for Self-knowledge must go on. This is why the Upaniṣad says again and again to keep up the habit of reading the scriptures, for when you do so you will not lose sight of the goal.

Ācāryāya priyam dhanam āhṛtya—give the teacher what he likes. The teacher has given you much knowledge. Now you must express your gratitude to him. He may also .be very poor. So do not give him useless things, things he does not want. If he needs food, give him food. If he needs clothes, then give him clothes. You can never say: 'I have paid my debt to my teacher. I don't owe him anything else.'

Prajātantum mā vyavacchetsīḥ—let there be no break in the family line. You have finished your education and are going back home. You are going to enter the householder's life. The teacher says it is your duty as a householder to marry and raise a family. Do not cut the family thread.

Dharmāt na pramaditavyam—never deviate from what is right. 'What is right' means what is good for all.

Kuśalāt means your own welfare, your well-being. *Bhūtyai* means prosperity. As a householder you have every right to seek prosperity. You need money. So the teacher says, 'Never deviate from seeking your own welfare or your own prosperity, but at the same time, you must do it by following truth and righteousness.'

देवपितृकार्याभ्यां न प्रमदितव्यम्। मातृदेवो भव।
पितृदेवो भव। आचार्यदेवो भव। अतिथिदेवो भव।

यान्यनवद्यानि कर्माणि। तानि सेवितव्यानि। नो इतराणि। यान्यस्माक सुचरितानि। तानि त्वयोपास्यानि॥ २॥

नो इतराणि। ये के चास्मच्छ्रेया सो ब्राह्मणाः। तेषां त्वयाऽऽसनेन प्रश्वसितव्यम्। श्रद्धया देयम्। अश्रद्धयाऽ-देयम्। श्रिया देयम्। ह्रिया देयम्। भिया देयम्। संविदा देयम्। अथ यदि ते कर्मविचिकित्सा वा वृत्तविचिकित्सा वा स्यात्॥ ३॥

ये तत्र ब्राह्मणाः संमर्शिनः। युक्ता आयुक्ताः। अलूक्षा धर्मकामाः स्युः। यथा ते तत्र वर्तेरन्। तथा तत्र वर्तेथाः। अथाभ्याख्यातेषु। ये तत्र ब्राह्मणाः संमर्शिनः। युक्ता आयुक्ताः। अलूक्षा धर्मकामाः स्युः। यथा ते तेषु वर्तेरन्। तथा तेषु वर्तेथाः। एष आदेशः। एष उपदेशः। एषा वेदोपनिषत्। एतदनुशासनम्। एवमुपासि-तव्यम्। एवमु चैतदुपास्यम्॥ ४॥ इति एकादशोऽनुवाकः॥

Devapitṛkāryābhyāṁ na pramaditavyam; Mātṛdevo bhava; Pitṛdevo bhava; Ācāryadevo bhava; Atithidevo bhava; Yānyanavadyāni karmāṇi; Tāni sevitavyāni; No itarāṇi; Yānyasmākaṁ sucaritāni; Tāni tvayopāsyāni.

No itarāṇi; Ye ke cāsmacchreyāṁso brāhmaṇāḥ; Teṣāṁ tvayā''sanena praśvasitavyam; Śraddhayā deyam; Aśraddhayā'deyam; Śriyā deyam; Hriyā deyam; Bhiyā deyam; Saṁvidā deyam; Atha yadi te karmavicikitsā vā vṛttavicikitsā vā syāt.

Ye tatra brāhmaṇāḥ sammarśinaḥ; Yuktā āyuktāḥ; Alūkṣā dharmakāmāḥ syuḥ; Yathā te tatra varteran; Tathā tatra vartethāḥ; Athābhyākhyāteṣu; Ye tatra brāhmaṇāḥ sammarśinaḥ; Yuktā āyuktāḥ; Alūkṣā dharmakāmāḥ syuḥ; Yathā te teṣu varteran; Tathā teṣu vartethāḥ; Eṣa ādeśaḥ; Eṣa upadeśaḥ; Eṣā vedopaniṣat; Etadanuśāsanam; Evamupāsitavyam; Evamu caitadupāsyam. Iti ekādaśo'nuvākaḥ.

Devapitṛkāryābhyām na pramaditavyam, do not neglect your duties to the gods and the ancestors; *mātṛdevaḥ bhava,* treat your mother as God; *pitṛdevaḥ bhava,* treat your father as God; *ācāryadevaḥ bhava,* treat your teacher as God; *atithidevaḥ bhava,* treat your guest as God; *yāni karmāṇi anavadyāni,* any work which is above reproach; *tāni sevitavyāni,* should be performed; *no itarāṇi,* no other [work]; *yāni asmākam sucaritāni,* anything good we [i.e., the teachers] do; *tāni tvayā upāsyāni,* you should perform.

Itarāṇi, other things [i.e., things not approved of by the scriptures, but being done by the teachers]; *na* [*upāsyāni*], should not be done; *ye ke ca brāhmaṇāḥ,* those brāhmins who; *asmāt śreyāmsaḥ,* are superior to us; *tvayā,* by you; *teṣām āsanena,* offering them seats; *praśvasitavyam,* they should thus be given relief; *śraddhayā deyam,* [when you give something to someone,] give with respect; *aśraddhayā adeyam,* if you cannot give with respect, then don't give at all; *śriyā deyam,* give gracefully; *hriyā deyam,* give with modesty; *bhiyā deyam,* give with fear [lest you offend]; *samvidā deyam,* give with goodwill; *atha yadi te karmavicikitsā vā vṛttavicikitsā vā syāt,* if you have any doubt in your mind about the propriety of what you are doing or the manner in which you are doing it.

Ye tatra brāhmaṇāḥ saṁmarśinaḥ, if there are wise brāhmins there at that time who; *yuktāḥ,* are devoted to their daily rituals; *āyuktāḥ,* are ready to do the right thing voluntarily; *alūkṣāḥ,* kind; *dharmakāmāḥ,* righteous; *syuḥ,* are present; *te tatra yathā varteran,* as they themselves behave there at that time, [you also]; *tatra tathā vartethāḥ,* behave there in the same way; *atha abhyākhyāteṣu,* then if someone questions what those people are doing; *ye tatra brāhmaṇāḥ saṁmarśinaḥ,* if there are wise brāhmins there at that time who; *yuktāḥ,* are devoted to their daily rituals; *āyuktāḥ,* are ready to do the right thing voluntarily; *alūkṣāḥ,* kind; *dharmakāmāḥ,* righteous; *syuḥ,* are present; *te teṣu yathā varteran,* as they themselves behave there at that time, [you also]; *tathā teṣu vartethāḥ,* behave there in the same way; *eṣaḥ ādeśaḥ,* this is the dictum; *eṣaḥ upadeśaḥ,* this is the instruction; *eṣā veda-upaniṣat,* this is the teaching of the Vedas; *etat anuśāsanam,* this is the principle; *evam upāsitavyam,* this is the ideal; *evam u ca etat upāsyam,* this is to be practised. *Iti ekādaśaḥ anuvākaḥ,* here ends the eleventh chapter.

2-4. Do not neglect your duties to the gods and the ancestors. Treat your mother as God. Treat your father as God. Treat your teacher as God. Treat your guest as God. Do only things no one can find fault with, and avoid other things. Anything good we [your teachers] do, you should also do, but other things we do [that are not approved of by the scriptures] you should not do. If there are brāhmins superior to us, you should offer them your seat and thus see to their comfort. When you give anything to anyone, give it with due respect. Never give anything without due respect. And when you give something, give it in the best manner possible. Give with humility and with fear, lest you offend the person to whom you are giving. And give with goodwill in your heart.

If you have any doubt in your mind about the propriety of what you are doing, or the manner in which you are doing it, then—if there are wise brāhmins there, who are devoted to their duties, who are ready to do the right thing voluntarily, who are kind, straightforward, and selfless—follow whatever they do. Again, if someone questions the propriety of what those people are doing, then—if there are wise brāhmins there, who are devoted to their duties, who are ready to do the right thing voluntarily, who are kind, straightforward, and selfless—follow whatever they do. This is the dictum, the advice, and the message of the Vedas. It is the command of God. This is the ideal. This is what should govern your conduct.

In those days, performing rites and rituals was a very important duty of a householder. These rituals were done in honour of different gods and goddesses and also of the family's ancestors. The Hindu idea is that we have an obligation to these deities and ancestors. We must remember and honour them every day. We must also live a good life for their sake. Suppose someone in your family was a very great saint. He expects that you will lead a good life, because it is your duty to follow the example and instructions of your ancestors and try to be like them. Similarly, there are certain gods and goddesses presiding over your family. They are watching what you are doing and protecting you. You must not let them down.

Mātṛ-devaḥ bhava. Pitṛ-devaḥ bhava. Here, the mother is honoured first. You should look upon her as a goddess, and you should regard your father as a god. The teacher also should be regarded as a deity. Your parents gave you your body, but the teacher has given you knowledge. He has helped your mind and intellect grow. Also, as a householder it is your duty to feed and look after guests. They should be treated with the highest respect, as if they are deities.

Then, the Upaniṣad says, do only those things which are *anavadyāni,* which are above reproach and will not bring you any blame—*no itarāṇi,* not other things. You should act so that no one can object to your behaviour. *Anavadya* could also mean beautiful or spotless. We should do only good things.

Yāni asmākam sucaritāni. The teacher is very humble. He says: 'We do many things. Follow us, but even while following us, follow only the good things we do. I may make mistakes. After all, I am a human being. But you must use your judgement. If I make mistakes, will you imitate me? So follow only the good things we do.' *Tāni tvayā upāsyāni*—only such things will you do. *No itarāṇi*—nothing else. You should respect your teacher and follow him. By and large, you should do what your teacher does. But if he does something wrong, you should not do it.

Ye ke ca asmāt śreyāṁsaḥ brāhmaṇāḥ. Suppose someone comes who is older or who is very respectable and is superior to you in learning or other qualities. Perhaps he is tired. You must offer him your seat. In other words, you must show him proper respect.

Śraddhayā deyam. Whatever you give, give with due respect. Never give anything *aśraddhayā,* with disrespect or contempt. If you give a person something carelessly or in a contemptuous manner, the person will be hurt or insulted. If you cannot give gladly, then it is better not to give at all. The manner of giving is very important.

So the teacher says, *'Śriyā deyam.'* Śaṅkara interprets this to mean that you should give as much as you can, according to your means. But it could also mean that you should give in a graceful manner. *Śriyā* can also mean beautifully or gracefully. The movement of your hands must be graceful so that the recipient feels happy to accept the gift. If you have seen offerings being made to the deity in a worship, you may have noticed how beautifully and artistically the worshipper moves his hands while making the offerings. So also, when you are presenting a gift to someone, you should feel that you are presenting it to God.

Hriyā deyam—give with shyness and humility, as if you are ashamed that you are not able to give more or to give something better. Some people feel very superior when they give: 'Oh, you want help? Here,

I have money, plenty of money. Come on.' That is not the way. Rather, you should think: 'Am I giving the right thing? Am I giving enough?'

In Burma you can see the Buddhist monks begging. They come with their bowls and stand before a house. But even before they come, the housewife is there outside waiting for them with a bowl of rice in her hands. And with what humility and respect she gives! So both are blessed. The giver and the recipient both feel happy.

In Hindu society one of the rules of charity is to give quietly. You should not let others know that you are giving. There was a story about a man who was always anxious to help the poor. He loved to give but he was always very apologetic about whatever he gave and sorry he could not give more. And he would always try to conceal his giving from others. He did not want anyone to know what he was doing. But there are some people who give and immediately want to see their names in the newspaper.

Bhiyā deyam—give with fear. Why fear? The idea is, you should feel you are standing before God so you must be careful. You should have a sense of fear lest you offend him or hurt him, lest you do not give in the correct manner. It also means that you should give with a sense of reverence.

Saṁvidā deyam. According to Śaṅkara, *saṁvidā* means *maitrī*—with goodwill, friendship, or affection. That is, you not only give the gift, but you also give your love and affection along with it.

We all know from experience that when food is served by a loved one, such as our mother, we enjoy it much more. Once Holy Mother asked one of her nieces to feed a Muslim young man named Amjad. But after some time she noticed that her niece was throwing the food from a distance onto the man's plate. She scolded the niece and said, 'Can anyone enjoy food when it is served like that?' Then she herself served the food.

Vicikitsā means a doubt. Suppose a doubt arises in your mind about *karma,* your duty, or about *vṛtti,* conduct. You don't know what is right or wrong. What should you do? The teacher says that there are people who are thoughtful, who use their own judgement. They do good things but not under compulsion (*āyuktāḥ*). They act independently and are not forced to do something. But they must be *alūkṣāḥ,* modest and gentle—not rude or haughty. And they should also be *dharmakāmāḥ,* religious-minded. The teacher says if you don't know what to do, follow what such a person does, one who is more noble and intelligent than you.

So the teacher says: 'This is the sum and substance of everything I have taught you. These are some basic guidelines which are the instructions of the teachers and of the scriptures. You are now going to begin the life of a householder, so you should follow these instructions.'

Chapter Twelve

शं नो मित्रः शं वरुणः। शं नो भवत्वर्यमा। शं न इन्द्रो बृहस्पतिः। शं नो विष्णुरुरुक्रमः। नमो ब्रह्मणे। नमस्ते वायो। त्वमेव प्रत्यक्षं ब्रह्मासि। त्वामेव प्रत्यक्षं ब्रह्मावादिषम्। ऋतमवादिषम्। सत्यमवादिषम्। तन्मामावीत्। तद्वक्तारमावीत्। आवीन्माम्। आवीद् वक्तारम्। ॐ शान्तिः शान्तिः शान्तिः॥ १॥ इति द्वादशोऽनुवाकः॥

Śaṁ no mitraḥ śaṁ varuṇaḥ; Śaṁ no bhavatvaryamā; Śaṁ na indro bṛhaspatiḥ; Śaṁ no viṣṇururukramaḥ; Namo brahmaṇe; Namaste vāyo; Tvameva pratyakṣaṁ brahmāsi; Tvāmeva pratyakṣaṁ brahmāvādiṣam; Ṛtam-avādiṣam; Satyamavādiṣam; Tanmāmāvīt; Tadvaktāram-āvīt; Āvīnmām; Āvīd vaktāram. Om Śāntiḥ Śāntiḥ Śāntiḥ. Iti dvādaśo'nuvākaḥ

[This prayer is the same as in Chapter One, except that here, the verbs in the second half of the verse are in the past tense.]

May Mitra, the Sun, be propitious to us. May Varuṇa be propitious to us. May Aryaman be propitious to us. May Indra be propitious to us. May Bṛhaspati be propitious to us. May Viṣṇu, who walks with long strides, be propitious to us. Salutations to Brahman.

Salutations to you, O Vāyu. You are no other than Brahman. I have declared that you are truly Brahman. I have declared that you are righteousness itself. I have declared that you are Truth. Brahman as Vāyu has protected me. He has protected the speaker. He has protected me. He has protected the speaker.

इति शीक्षावल्ली समाप्ता ॥

Iti śīkṣāvallī samāptā.

Here ends the Śīkṣā-vallī.

PART TWO

BRAHMĀNANDA-VALLĪ

Chapter One

ॐ सह नाववतु। सह नौ भुनक्तु। सह वीर्यं करवावहै। तेजस्वि नावधीतमस्तु मा विद्विषावहै॥

ॐ शान्तिः शान्तिः शान्तिः॥

Om. Saha nāvavatu; Saha nau bhunaktu; Saha vīryaṁ karavāvahai; Tejasvi nāvadhītamastu mā vidviṣāvahai. Om Śāntih Śāntiḥ Śāntiḥ.

[May Brahman] *nau,* us [both the teacher and the student]; *saha,* equally; *avatu,* protect; *nau,* both of us; *saha,* equally; *bhunaktu,* give us [the benefit of the learning]; *saha,* equally; *vīryam karavāvahai,* [may we] apply ourselves [for the benefit of the learning]; *nau,* of us both; *adhītam,* the learning; *tejasvi,* fruitful; *astu,* be; *mā vidviṣāvahai,* may we never be jealous of each other; *śāntiḥ,* [may there be] peace [in one's body and mind]; *śāntiḥ,* [may there be] peace [in the elements]; *śāntiḥ,* [may there be] peace [in the animal world].

May Brahman protect us both equally. May it also give us equally the benefit of the learning. May we both work equally hard to learn. May what we learn be equally fruitful. May we never be jealous of each other. Om Peace! Peace! Peace!

Saha nau avatu. The teacher and the student are both praying: Please protect us—both of us.

Saha nau bhunaktu. Together may we benefit from this study. See that we can derive the best results, that we can both reap the fruits of our study together. The word *bhunaktu* comes from the root *bhuj,* 'to enjoy.' Let us enjoy together. The student and the teacher should both enjoy the study of the Upaniṣad.

Saha vīryam karavāvahai. Make us both strong and vigorous so that we can apply ourselves to this study.

Tejasvi nau adhītam astu. May our study be vigorous, not indifferent, not half-hearted. Let us study enthusiastically. May our understanding also be deep.

Mā vidviṣāvahai. Sometimes the teacher-student relationship gets strained, or even embittered. So this is the prayer: Let us have a very cordial relationship. If there is a good relationship, if the teacher and the student love each other, then they can progress. Suppose the students are indifferent. How can the teacher teach them? He can't. Or suppose a teacher has a brilliant student who asks him difficult questions that he cannot answer. He may become jealous of that student. So they pray: Let us have a good relationship. Let us love each other and help each other.

ॐ ब्रह्मविदाप्नोति परम्। तदेषाऽभ्युक्ता। सत्यं ज्ञानमनन्तं ब्रह्म। यो वेद निहितं गुहायां परमे व्योमन्। सोऽश्नुते सर्वान् कामान् सह। ब्रह्मणा विपश्चितेति।

तस्माद्वा एतस्मादात्मन आकाशः संभूतः। आकाशाद्वायुः। वायोरग्निः। अग्नेरापः। अद्भ्यः पृथिवी। पृथिव्या ओषधयः। ओषधीभ्योऽन्नम्। अन्नात्पुरुषः। स वा एष पुरुषोऽन्नरसमयः। तस्येदमेव शिरः। अयं दक्षिणः पक्षः। अयमुत्तरः पक्षः। अयमात्मा। इदं पुच्छं प्रतिष्ठा। तदप्येष श्लोको भवति॥ १॥ इति प्रथमोऽनुवाकः॥

Om. Brahmavidāpnoti param; Tadeṣā'bhyuktā; Satyaṁ jñānamanantaṁ brahma; Yo veda nihitaṁ guhāyāṁ parame vyoman; So'śnute sarvān kāmān saha; Brahmaṇā vipaściteti.

Tasmādvā etasmādātmana ākāśaḥ saṁbhūtaḥ; Ākāśādvāyuḥ; Vāyoragniḥ; Agnerāpaḥ; Adbhyaḥ pṛthivī; Pṛthivyā oṣadhayaḥ; Oṣadhībhyo'nnam; Annātpuruṣaḥ; Sa vā eṣa puruṣo'nnarasamayaḥ; Tasyedameva śiraḥ; Ayaṁ dakṣiṇaḥ pakṣaḥ; Ayamuttaraḥ pakṣaḥ; Ayamātmā; Idaṁ pucchaṁ pratiṣṭhā; Tadapyeṣa śloko bhavati. Iti prathamo'nuvākaḥ.

[1] *Brahmavit paraṁ āpnoti,* he who knows the biggest attains Para Brahman, the highest reward possible; *tat eṣā abhyuktā,* this is what a Ṛk mantra says on the subject; *brahma,* Brahman [is]; *satyam jñānam*

anantam, Truth [i.e., it is always the same], Knowledge itself, Infinite; [*brahma*] *yaḥ parame vyoman guhāyām nihitam veda,* he who knows [Brahman, the Self, earlier described as *satyam jñānam anantam*] lying in the sublime cave of the heart; *saḥ aśnute,* he enjoys; *sarvān kāmān saha,* along with all the things a person wishes to enjoy; *vipaścitā brahmaṇā,* the status of the omniscient Brahman.

Tasmāt vai etasmāt ātmanaḥ, from that Self [i.e., Brahman]; *ākāśaḥ sambhūtaḥ,* came space; *ākāśāt,* from space; *vāyuḥ,* [came] air; *vāyoḥ agniḥ,* from air [came] fire; *agneḥ,* from fire; *āpaḥ,* water; *adbhyaḥ,* from water; *pṛthivī,* earth; *pṛthivyāḥ,* from earth; *oṣadhayaḥ,* plants and herbs; *oṣadhībhyaḥ,* from plants and herbs; *annam,* food; *annāt,* from food; *puruṣaḥ,* a human being; *saḥ vai eṣaḥ puruṣaḥ anna-rasa-mayaḥ,* that human being is the by-product of food; *tasya idam eva śiraḥ,* this is the head of that [human being]; *ayam dakṣiṇaḥ pakṣaḥ,* this [i.e., the right arm] is the right wing; *ayam uttaraḥ pakṣaḥ,* this [the left arm] is the left wing; *ayam,* this [the trunk of the body]; *ātmā,* the self [the central part of the body]; *idam,* this [the lower part of the body]; *puccham pratiṣṭhā,* the tail that supports; *tat api eṣaḥ ślokaḥ bhavati,* there is a verse about this. *Iti prathamaḥ anuvākaḥ,* here ends the first chapter.

1. He who knows Brahman, knows, in fact, Para Brahman. Here is a mantra on the subject: Brahman is Truth, Knowledge, Infinity. It is in the space within the heart [i.e., the intellect], which is like a cave. He who realizes the Self there not only realizes the

all-knowing Brahman, but also attains everything he wants.

From this Self comes space; from space, air; from air, fire; from fire, water; from water, earth; from earth, plants and herbs; from plants and herbs, food; and from food comes a human being. A human being is, in fact, a product of food. There is a head for that human being. His right arm is the right wing, the left arm is the left wing, the trunk is the middle part of the body, and the lower part of the body is the tail that supports the body. There is a verse about this:

Why should we try to know Brahman? Is there any advantage in knowing Brahman? The answer is: *Brahmavit āpnoti param*—he who knows Brahman attains the highest. It is the supreme attainment. The Upaniṣad is giving an inducement, as it were.

The ancient seers have said that Brahman is *satyam jñānam anantam*—truth, knowledge, and infinity. It is not that these are qualities of Brahman. An object and its quality are two different things. For instance, you may say, 'Here is a white flower.' Whiteness is the quality that is superimposed on the flower. But this quality of whiteness might be superimposed on any other object. Or again, this flower is white, but another might be red. Here, however, the adjectives do not limit Brahman. Brahman is Truth itself, Knowledge itself, and Infinity itself.

And it is not that at one time Brahman is *satyam,* and at another time it is *jñānam,* and at still another time *anantam.* No, it is always *satyam jñānam anantam*—simultaneously.

As we are human beings with limited minds, we cannot conceive of something infinite, without a form, which cannot be perceived by the senses. That is why we need to use some words of reference. But all the time we know that Brahman is not limited by such words.

But where is Brahman? *Nihitam guhāyām. Guhā* means a cave. Here, it means the heart. If something is inside a cave, it is difficult to see it. So Brahman is hidden within the heart. He is the inmost being of all of us, the essence of everything. Śaṅkara says that the word *guhā* also refers to the intellect, because we understand things through the intellect.

The word *nihitam* has two meanings. *Hitam* means residing. *Ni* is very significant. It could mean *nitya,* always—not just now or in a moment or two. He is always residing in the heart. He is eternally present, and present as the inmost being of everything. *Ni* could also mean *nigūḍhatvena*—in the depths. He resides in the deepest core of everything. He is deep in the heart. Without Brahman we cannot exist.

Guhā, the heart, is also called *parama vyoma. Vyoma* is space. It is the same as *ākāśa.* We often use the term *hṛdaya ākāśa,* the space in the heart. If I am to experience Brahman, where shall I experience it? Is Brahman an object outside of me that I can see it or touch it? No. Brahman is right within me, within my heart. The heart is called *parama,* sacred, or supreme, because that is where we have the sacred experience of Brahman. But when we have this experience, we realize that the space within us is also the space without. In other words, we realize we are one with everything.

Sarvān kāmān aśnute. When a person realizes Brahman, he enjoys everything. Whatever joys there are, all these put together are not equal to the satisfaction that you derive from this experience. When you have this experience you have a sense of fulfilment that fills every nook and corner of your being. Śaṅkara says it is not a gradual process. It is not that one enjoyment comes after another. It is *saha,* altogether. You are suddenly flooded.

Suppose there is a powerful light but it is enclosed by different layers of coverings. The light will then be very weak. That is our condition now. We are now identified with the coverings of our body and other things, so we experience very little bliss. But if somehow or other we manage to break through those coverings, we will suddenly be flooded with light. Brahman, the Self, is shining within. Now its light is feeble. But if we are able to realize Brahman, we attain Brahmānanda, the bliss of Brahman. The joy we experience then is overwhelming. It is the sum total of all joys.

Then the Upaniṣad gives a description of the evolution of the universe—how things evolve from fine to gross. This is, perhaps, what Sri Aurobindo would describe as *descent.* First there is Brahman, Brahman everywhere. Brahman at this stage is *nirguṇa nirākāra*—without qualities, without a form. You cannot say what it is like. The first manifestation then is space (*ākāśa*). Space is also all-pervasive. From space comes air (*vāyu*), from air comes fire (*agni*), from fire come water (*āpa*), and then from water comes earth (*pṛthivī*).

Then, from the earth, vegetation (*oṣadhaya*) grows, and this vegetation produces food (*anna*). Then living beings (*puruṣa*) are manifested. Food must come first, because there cannot be any life without food. The body is said to be *annarasamaya,* made of the essence of food. It is nothing but food. This food passes in a seed form from the parents to the child, and from that the body is made. The body is also compared to molten copper poured into a mould, because we are the image of our parents. The copper is the seed of the food from the parents.

Śaṅkara says that the word *puruṣa* here refers to human beings because human beings are superior. Human beings, he says, are distinguished from animals by two things: *jñāna,* knowledge, and *karma,* actions. We can understand and learn, and we can pass our knowledge on to another generation. And we can also discriminate in our actions. We can decide what we should do: 'I will do this, but I will not do that.'

Then the Upaniṣad compares the human body to a bird. Perhaps in the course of evolution we were at one time birds. Our right and left arms are compared to wings, and the lower part of our body is compared to the tail. The tail is called the *pratiṣṭhā,* the support, because without the tail a bird cannot fly. The whole body is balanced, like an airplane. If a wing or the tail of the plane goes, then the plane cannot fly.

So this is a description of the *annamaya kośa,* the human body.

Chapter Two

अन्नाद्वै प्रजाः प्रजायन्ते। याः काश्च पृथिवीꣳश्रिताः। अथो अन्नेनैव जीवन्ति। अथैनदपि यन्त्यन्ततः। अन्नꣳ हि भूतानां ज्येष्ठम्। तस्मात् सर्वौषधमुच्यते। सर्वं वै तेऽन्नमाप्नुवन्ति। येऽन्नं ब्रह्मोपासते। अन्नꣳ हि भूतानां ज्येष्ठम्। तस्मात् सर्वौषधमुच्यते। अन्नाद् भूतानि जायन्ते। जातान्यन्नेन वर्धन्ते। अद्यतेऽत्ति च भूतानि। तस्मादन्नं तदुच्यत इति।

तस्माद्वा एतस्मादन्नरसमयात्। अन्योऽन्तर आत्मा प्राणमयः। तेनैष पूर्णः। स वा एष पुरुषविध एव। तस्य पुरुषविधताम्। अन्वयं पुरुषविधः। तस्य प्राण एव शिरः। व्यानो दक्षिणः पक्षः। अपान उत्तरः पक्षः। आकाश आत्मा। पृथिवी पुच्छं प्रतिष्ठा। तदप्येष श्लोको भवति॥ १ ॥ इति द्वितीयोऽनुवाकः॥

Annādvai prajāḥ prajāyante; Yāḥ kāśca pṛthivīṁ-śritāḥ; Atho annenaiva jīvanti; Athainadapi yantyantataḥ;

Annaṁ hi bhūtānāṁ jyeṣṭham; Tasmāt sarvauṣadhamucyate; Sarvaṁ vai te'nnamāpnuvanti; Ye'nnaṁ brahmopāsate; Annaṁ hi bhūtānāṁ jyeṣṭham; Tasmāt sarvauṣadhamucyate; Annād bhūtāni jāyante; Jātānyannena vardhante; Adyate'tti ca bhūtāni; Tasmādannaṁ taducyata iti.

Tasmādvā etasmādannarasamayāt; Anyo'ntara ātmā prāṇamayaḥ; Tenaiṣa pūrṇaḥ; Sa vā eṣa puruṣavidha eva; Tasya puruṣavidhatām; Anvayaṁ puruṣavidhaḥ; Tasya prāṇa eva śiraḥ; Vyāno dakṣiṇaḥ pakṣaḥ; Apāna uttaraḥ pakṣaḥ; Ākāśa ātmā; Pṛthivī pucchaṁ pratiṣṭhā; Tadapyeṣa śloko bhavati. Iti dvitīyo'nuvākaḥ.

Yāḥ kāḥ ca prajāḥ pṛthivīm śritāḥ, whatever living things are in this world; *annāt vai prajāyante,* [all of them] are products of food; *atha annena eva jīvanti,* they are also sustained by food; *atha,* moreover; *antataḥ,* in the end [when they die]; *enat apiyanti,* they dissolve into this [food]; *hi,* for; *annam,* [this] food; *bhūtānām jyeṣṭham,* is the forerunner of living things; *tasmāt,* this is why; *sarvausadham ucyate,* [food] is called the remedy for all ailments [hunger, etc.]; *ye,* those who; *annam brahma upāsate,* wōrship food as Brahman [i.e., as the source, the support, and the end of every living thing]; *te,* they; *sarvam annam vai āpnuvanti,* attain all the food [i.e., all objects of pleasure] that exists; *hi,* since; *annam bhūtānām jyeṣṭham,* food comes before all living beings; *tasmāt sarvauṣadham ucyate,* that is why it is called the remedy for all ailments of living beings [it is like possessing all sense pleasures]; *annāt bhūtāni jāyante,* living beings come from food; *jātāni annena vardhante,* being born, they grow on food; *adyate,* it is eaten [by living beings]; *ca atti bhūtāni,* living beings themselves are in their turn eaten by it [the so-called food]; *tasmāt,* that is why; *tat annam ucyate iti,* it is called *anna,* food [the word *anna* is derived from the root *ad,* which means 'to eat'].

Tasmāt vai etasmāt annarasamayāt anyaḥ, different from the aforesaid body made from food [but]; *antaraḥ,* inside [that body]; *prāṇamayaḥ,* in the form of air; *ātmā,* you feel as part of your self [it is like a separate sheath]; *tena,* by this [sheath of air, the prāṇamaya kośa]; *eṣaḥ,* this [gross body—i.e., the annamaya kośa]; *pūrṇaḥ,* is filled; *saḥ vai eṣaḥ,* this [sheath of prāṇa, the prāṇamaya kośa]; *puruṣavidhaḥ eva,* looks exactly like a human body [complete with all its limbs]; *tasya,* of that [gross body]; *puruṣavidhatam,* in the form of a human body; *anu,* copy; *ayam,* this [prāṇamaya kośa]; *puruṣavidhaḥ,* body in the shape of a human being; *tasya,* of this [prāṇamaya kośa]; *prāṇaḥ eva,* the breath [passing through the mouth and the nostrils]; *śiraḥ,* is the head; *vyānaḥ dakṣiṇaḥ pakṣaḥ,* vyāna [the air that pervades the whole body] is the right wing; *apānaḥ uttaraḥ pakṣaḥ,* apāna [the air that is exhaled] is the left wing; *ākāśaḥ ātmā,* ākāśa [i.e., samāna, the vital breath that helps digest food] is the trunk; *pṛthivī,* the deity supporting the body [i.e., udāna, which keeps the body from rising in the air]; *puccham pratiṣṭhā,* is the tail that keeps the body in balance; *tat api eṣaḥ ślokaḥ bhavati,* there is a verse about this. *Iti dvitīyaḥ anuvākaḥ,* here ends the second chapter.

1. Whatever living beings exist in this world are products of food. They are also sustained by food, and in the end they dissolve into food. This is because food preceded them. For this reason, food is called the remedy for all ills of living beings. Those who worship food as Brahman [i.e., as the origin, the support, and the end of all living beings] get all the food that there is. Food precedes living beings. That is why it is said that food is the remedy for all ills [and that all the food that exists is at their command]. Living beings are born from food, and they are sustained by food. Food is consumed by living beings, and living beings themselves are consumed by food. That is why food is called *anna,* that which eats.

There is a self separate from the self produced by food [the annamaya kośa] mentioned earlier. It is inside the sheath of food and is called the *prāṇamaya kośa* [because it is all air and it is in the form of a sheath]. It fills the gross body made of food and has the same human form. The prāṇamaya kośa in the form of a human body is an exact copy of the annamaya kośa in the form of a human body. Prāṇa [the in-coming breath] is the head; vyāna [the air that goes all over the body] is the right wing; apāna [the out-going breath] is the left wing; ākāśa [i.e., samāna, the vital breath that digests food] is the trunk; and earth [i.e., udāna, the vital breath that gives us balance] maintains balance in the body. There is a verse on this subject:

All living beings come from food and are sustained by food. Without food we cannot exist. In India now tigers and other animals have almost become extinct because they cannot get food. Life multiplies and goes on because of food.

Then again, when we die we become food. Our bodies are eaten by worms, insects, and other creatures. We came from food, we are sustained by food, and in the end we go back into food. This is the cycle.

Food is called *jyeṣṭham,* the first cause of, or the pre-condition for, all beings. *Bhūtānām* means living beings. The Hindu scriptures say there are four kinds of living beings: *jarāyuja,* those born from the womb; *aṇḍaja,* those born from eggs; *svedaja,* those born from moisture (in those days people thought that insects such as mosquitoes were born directly from water); and *udbhijja,* plants, which are born from the earth. All these living beings must have food. Otherwise they cannot live.

Food is also called *sarvauṣadham,* because it is the panacea for all beings. It cures our hunger and thirst, and gives us relief.

Suppose a person worships *annam,* food, as Brahman. What it means is that he worships this body. To many people, this body is their first and last concern. It is supreme and is the only reality to them. What happens to such a person? He gets what he wants. If you worship the body, then you will get a good, healthy body. If you know nothing beyond the body, naturally all your progress will centre round your body.

But why does the Upaniṣad talk about meditating on the gross body as Brahman? Śaṅkara says you have to start somewhere. Each sheath is Brahman, but not the Supreme Brahman. The gross body is the starting point, but slowly you transcend it. You go from the gross body to a finer body, and then again to another finer body, and so on till you reach the Self.

Why is food called *annam?* The word *annam* comes from the root *ad,* to eat. The Upaniṣad says that we eat food and food eats us, both. We support ourselves by eating food, and then we become converted into food for others.

This body is called *annarasa,* the essence of food, because it is nothing but a transformation of food. Whatever we eat becomes transformed into muscles, bones, blood, and other things. The annamaya kośa is also called the *sthūla śarīra,* the gross body. Within this gross body is the *sūkṣma śarīra,* the subtle body. The subtle body consists of several layers. The first is the *prāṇamaya kośa,* the sheath of the vital breath. The next is the *manomaya kośa,* the sheath of the mind. And the last is the *vijñānamaya kośa,* the sheath of the intellect. They go from gross to fine. Then beyond this subtle body, and finer, there is the *ānandamaya kośa,* the sheath of bliss.

These are actually different layers of our personality. Sometimes we live on the gross level, and we get joy from eating good food. Sometimes we are on the mental level, and are thoughtful and imaginative. And at other times we are on the intellectual level and we love books and scholarship. For all these levels we need some external support. But when we are on the level of the ānandamaya kośa, there is nothing but bliss. We are not aware that we have a body or mind or intellect. And there is nothing external that supports that bliss. We are completely absorbed within ourself.

When people say they have seen a spirit, or ghost, it is the sūkṣma śarīra, the subtle body, of a person that they have seen. Not all ghosts are harmful. When Swami Brahmananda was in Vrindaban, he used to get up during the night and meditate, and he would see the ghost of a saint meditating next to him. One night he overslept. The ghost then pushed him and said: 'Get up. It's time to meditate.'

The Upaniṣad now discusses the prāṇamaya kośa, the sheath of prāṇa, the vital breath. It says it is inside and separate from this gross body. The Upaniṣad calls it the *ātmā.* It is like the individual self, the soul, of the gross body.

This prāṇa is not just in one part of the body. It is everywhere, in all parts of the body. It fills it. Śaṅkara compares it to a bellows. When a blacksmith is melting something he uses a bellows to pump air at the fire to make it burn well. The air fills every part of the bellows. Similarly, air fills every part of the gross body.

The prāṇamaya kośa is also shaped like the human body (*puruṣavidhaḥ*). Śaṅkara says it is like something cast in a mould. If you pour molten copper into a mould, the copper takes the same shape as the mould. The prāṇamaya kośa is like the molten copper.

Though this prāṇa is all over the body, it has five different functions. These five functions are called: *prāṇa, apāna, vyāna, udāna,* and *samāna.* The Upaniṣad compares these five functions of prāṇa to the different parts of a bird. Prāṇa, our inhaling, goes upwards, so it is compared to the head (*śiraḥ*). Apāna is the function of exhaling. It goes through the left nostril and is compared to the left wing (*uttaraḥ pakṣaḥ*) of the bird. Vyāna pervades the whole body and is called the right wing (*dakṣiṇaḥ pakṣaḥ*). Samāna helps digest the food we eat, so it is compared to the trunk. And udāna supports us and gives us balance, so it is called the tail (*puccham*). Without udāna, the body would be jolted upwards, or it would drop down to the earth by its own weight.

Why has this idea of kośas, or sheaths, been introduced? Śaṅkara compares the Self within to a grain of rice. Just as we have to remove the husks to get to the grain of rice, so also, we first have to remove the different coverings of our personality before we can get to the Self.

Śaṅkara says the Self is the inmost. It is like going to see a king in a palace. There is one room within another room within another room that you have to go through. Finally you get to the inmost room and see the occupant of the palace, the king. These rooms are the kośas, and the king is the Self. Yet another example is that the kośas are like a sheath that covers a sword, and the Self is like the sword.

Chapter Three

प्राणं देवा अनु प्राणन्ति। मनुष्याः पशवश्च ये। प्राणो हि भूतानामायुः। तस्मात् सर्वायुषमुच्यते। सर्वमेव त आयुर्यन्ति। ये प्राणं ब्रह्मोपासते। प्राणो हि भूतानामायुः। तस्मात् सर्वायुषमुच्यत इति।

तस्यैष एव शारीर आत्मा। यः पूर्वस्य। तस्माद्वा एतस्मात् प्राणमयात्। अन्योऽन्तर आत्मा मनोमयः। तेनैष पूर्णः। स वा एष पुरुषविध एव। तस्य पुरुषविधताम्। अन्वयं पुरुषविधः। तस्य यजुरेव शिरः। ऋग्दक्षिणः पक्षः। सामोत्तरः पक्षः। आदेश आत्मा। अथर्वाङ्गिरसः पुच्छं प्रतिष्ठा। तदप्येष श्लोको भवति॥ १॥ इति तृतीयोऽनुवाकः॥

Prāṇaṁ devā anu prāṇanti; Manuṣyāḥ paśavaśca ye; Prāṇo hi bhūtānāmāyuḥ; Tasmāt sarvāyuṣamucyate; Sarvameva ta āyuryanti; Ye prāṇaṁ brahmopāsate; Prāṇo hi bhūtānāmāyuḥ; Tasmāt sarvāyuṣamucyata iti.

Tasyaiṣa eva śārīra ātmā; Yaḥ pūrvasya; Tasmādvā etasmāt prāṇamayāt; Anyo'ntara ātmā manomayaḥ; Tenaiṣa pūrṇaḥ; Sa vā eṣa puruṣavidha eva; Tasya puruṣavidhatām; Anvayaṁ puruṣavidhaḥ; Tasya yajur-eva śiraḥ; Ṛgdakṣiṇaḥ pakṣaḥ; Sāmottaraḥ pakṣaḥ;

Ādeśa ātmā; Atharvāṅgirasaḥ puccham pratiṣṭhā; Tad-apyeṣa śloko bhavati. Iti tṛtīyo'nuvākaḥ.

Devāḥ, the organs; *prāṇam,* the self as prāṇa, the vital breath; *anu prāṇanti,* are inspired by the principle of prāṇa and are thereby able to perform their duties; [*tathā*] *ye manuṣyāḥ,* the same principle applies to human beings; *paśavaḥ ca,* as well as to beasts; *hi,* that is why; *prāṇaḥ bhūtānām āyuḥ,* prāṇa is responsible for the life of all beings; *tasmāt sarvāyuṣam ucyate,* for this reason it is called 'the life of all lives'; *ye prāṇam brahma upāsate,* people who worship prāṇa as Brahman; *te sarvam eva āyuḥ yanti,* attain the full span of life; *hi prāṇaḥ bhūtānām āyuḥ,* prāṇa is the life of all beings; *tasmāt sarvāyuṣam ucyate iti,* and that is why it is called 'the life of all lives.'

Tasya pūrvasya yaḥ eṣaḥ eva śārīraḥ ātmā, this [the prāṇamaya kośa] is the in-dwelling self of the aforesaid [annamaya kośa]; *tasmāt etasmāt prāṇamayāt vai anyaḥ antaraḥ ātmā manomayaḥ,* there is another self deeper than this called the manomaya kośa [the mental sheath]; *tena,* by that [the mind, or manomaya kośa]; *eṣaḥ,* this [the prāṇamaya kośa]; *pūrṇaḥ,* is filled; *saḥ eṣaḥ vai puruṣavidhaḥ eva,* this [manomaya] self also has a human form; *tasya puruṣavidhatām anu ayam puruṣavidhaḥ,* in the way that [i.e., the prāṇamaya self] has a human form, in the same way this [the manomaya self] also has a human form; *yajuḥ eva tasya śiraḥ,* the Yajuḥ mantra is its head; *ṛg dakṣiṇaḥ pakṣaḥ,* the Ṛg mantra is its right wing; *sāma uttaraḥ pakṣaḥ,* the Sāma is its left wing; *ādeśaḥ,* the brāhmaṇa part of the Vedas;

ātmā, is the middle part of the body; *atharvāṅgirasaḥ pratiṣṭhā puccham,* the Atharva Aṅgirasa is its tail; *tat api eṣaḥ ślokaḥ bhavati,* here is a verse on the subject. *Iti tṛtīyaḥ anuvākaḥ,* here ends the third chapter.

1. The organs follow prāṇa, and that enables them to perform their respective duties. Whether they are organs of human beings or organs of animals, the same principle holds good. Prāṇa gives life to all living beings. This is why prāṇa is called *sarvāyuṣam,* the life of all living beings. Those who worship prāṇa as Brahman attain the full span of life. Since all living beings get their life from prāṇa, it is called *sarvāyuṣam,* the life of all living beings. This prāṇa is the indwelling self of the annamaya kośa, the sheath of food, mentioned earlier.

Deeper than the prāṇamaya kośa is the manomaya kośa, the sheath of the mind. This manomaya kośa fills the entire prāṇamaya kośa. The manomaya kośa also has a human form. Just as the prāṇamaya kośa has a human form, in the same way the manomaya kośa has a human form. The Yajuḥ is its head, the Ṛk is its right wing, and the Sāma is its left wing. The Brāhmaṇa part is the middle of the body, and the Atharva Aṅgirasa is its tail. There is the following verse on the subject:

The word *deva* means that which is shining, that which is luminous. It ordinarily refers to a deity. But here the word means the sense organs. Why? Because the sense organs illuminate objects for us.

Without eyes I cannot see anything. It is as if the eyes throw light on an object and reveal it to me.

But suppose someone has died, and you find that all his senses are still intact. His eyes are still good, his ears are still good, and so on, but they do not function. What is lacking? Prāṇa, the vital force. Prāṇa gives life to our sense organs. If there is no life in a person, then the sense organs cannot function. Prāṇa is the life of all living beings, not just human beings.

The Upaniṣad says that if you worship prāṇa as Brahman you attain the full span of life (*sarvāyuḥ*). *Āyuḥ* here means span of life. According to Śaṅkara, the full span of life is one hundred years (*śata varṣāṇi*). However, this cannot be taken literally. The idea is that you get whatever you want. If you concentrate on a particular idea, you can easily get it. Śaṅkara says: '*Yadguṇakaṁ brahmopāste sa tadguṇabhāgbhavati.* If a person worships Brahman as being of a particular quality, he attains that quality.' Brahman is the embodiment of everything, so if you worship Brahman as beauty, you will acquire beauty. Or if you worship Brahman as courage, purity, or knowledge, you will acquire one of those qualities. You will become like Brahman.

The question is, what will you do with your life? If a person feels that life has no purpose, then his life is certainly wasted. We must think: 'I want to live so that I can finish my task of knowing who I am. I want to realize the Self. This is the purpose of life. I do not want to die until I attain that.'

Inside the prāṇamaya kośa is the manomaya kośa, the sheath of the mind. Just as the prāṇamaya kośa completely fills the sheath of food (the annamaya kośa), so also, the manomaya kośa fills the sheath of prāṇa. And it also has the same form.

Again the Upaniṣad uses the illustration of a bird. Here, the most important part, the head, is given to the Yajur Veda. Why is the Yajur Veda compared to the head of the bird? The Yajur Veda is the Veda in which the mantras are in irregular metre. The Sāma Veda is very musical and can be sung. In fact, Indian music is supposed to have originated in the Sāma Veda. But the Yajur Veda cannot be sung. Nevertheless, it is considered very important. Śaṅkara explains that it is because most of the rituals are based on the Yajur Veda, and most of the mantras that are recited during the rituals when oblations are offered are from the Yajur Veda. The Yajur Veda takes you through the *karma kāṇḍa,* the ritualistic portion of the Vedas.

Though Śaṅkara is always saying that you can only attain liberation through knowledge, you cannot dismiss the karma kāṇḍa altogether. If you have desires you must overcome them somehow or other. So long as you have desires you have to perform certain duties for purifying the mind. Through karma you can have a long life, plenty of money, and you can also attain the heavenly realm. But gradually, when you perform the duties that the Vedas prescribe, you attain *citta-śuddhi,* purification of the mind. At that time some understanding comes that when you have desires, you suffer, because this world is ephemeral. Then the desire comes for that which never decays, which is permanent. You reject all enjoyments in this world and the next and you seek Self-knowledge.

Why are the Vedas connected with the manomaya kośa? Śaṅkara explains that when you recite the mantras of the Vedas, it is not just a physical exercise. It is mental. Many of us practise *japam,* repetition of a mantra. Now this japam must be done through the mind. There must be a mental reaction, or feeling, in the mind. So also, in the case of the Vedas, the words have a meaning. When you understand their meaning, it evokes certain thoughts in your mind. You contemplate the meaning of the words, and as you contemplate, there is a reaction in your mind. Some feelings arise in your mind (*manovṛtti*). Then this is repeated again and again. When you go on repeating the mantras like this, what was at first only an abstract thought or idea becomes transformed and concretized, as it were. The immediate result is that you attain a long life or money or some such thing. But the ultimate result is destruction of ignorance and Self-knowledge.

Śaṅkara also quotes from a scripture that says: *'Sarve vedā yatraikaṁ bhavanti sa mānasīna ātmā*—All the Vedas have one purpose [i.e., they agree on one thing]—the Self is in the mind.' Self-knowledge is the goal of all the Vedas, whether you are performing rituals of the karma kāṇḍa or you are seeking knowledge from the jñāna kāṇḍa, whether you are studying the

Ṛg Veda, the Sāma Veda, or some other Veda. The karma kāṇḍa may take you in a roundabout way, but eventually, through the performance of the rituals, you outgrow them and you discover you don't need them any longer.

The brāhmaṇa portion of the Vedas is called the trunk, because that is the part of the Vedas in which the instructions are given as to how to perform the rites and rituals. As they are issued like orders, they are called *ādeśa,* orders. And the instructions by Atharva and the sages named Aṅgirasa are called the *puccham,* the tail. These instructions, Śaṅkara says, pertain to rituals through which you acquire peace, prosperity, and the like (*śāntikapauṣṭikādi*). They support life, so they are like the tail which gives support.

Chapter Four

यतो वाचो निवर्तन्ते। अप्राप्य मनसा सह। आनन्दं ब्रह्मणो विद्वान्। न बिभेति कदाचनेति।

तस्यैष एव शारीर आत्मा। यः पूर्वस्य। तस्माद्वा एतस्मान्मनोमयात्। अन्योऽन्तर आत्मा विज्ञानमयः। तेनैष पूर्णः। स वा एष पुरुषविध एव। तस्य पुरुषविधताम्। अन्वयं पुरुषविधः। तस्य श्रद्धैव शिरः। ऋतं दक्षिणः पक्षः। सत्यमुत्तरः पक्षः। योग आत्मा। महः पुच्छं

प्रतिष्ठा। तदप्येष श्लोको भवति॥ १॥ इति चतुर्थोऽनुवाकः॥

Yato vāco nivartante; Aprāpya manasā saha; Ānandaṁ brahmaṇo vidvān; Na bibheti kadācaneti.

Tasyaiṣa eva śārīra ātmā; Yaḥ pūrvasya; Tasmādvā etasmānmanomayāt; Anyo'ntara ātmā vijñānamayaḥ; Tenaiṣa pūrṇaḥ; Sa vā eṣa puruṣavidha eva; Tasya puruṣavidhatām; Anvayaṁ puruṣavidhaḥ; Tasya śraddhaiva śiraḥ; Ṛtaṁ dakṣiṇaḥ pakṣaḥ; Satyamuttaraḥ pakṣaḥ; Yoga ātmā; Mahaḥ pucchaṁ pratiṣṭhā; Tadapyeṣa śloko bhavati. Iti caturtho'nuvākaḥ.

Vācaḥ, words; *manasā saha,* together with thoughts; *aprāpya,* unable to reach; *yataḥ,* from that [Brahman]; *nivartante,* return; *brahmaṇaḥ vidvān ānandam,* he who knows Brahman enjoys bliss; *kadācana na bibheti,* is never afraid [of anyone or anything].

Tasya pūrvasya yaḥ eṣaḥ eva śārīraḥ ātmā, this [manomaya] is the indwelling self of the aforesaid [prāṇamaya]; *tasmāt vai etasmāt manomayāt anyaḥ antaraḥ ātmā,* deeper within this manomaya kośa is another self; *vijñānamayaḥ,* [called] the vijñānamaya kośa [the sheath of the intellect]; *tena eṣaḥ pūrṇaḥ,* by that [vijñānamaya kośa] this [manomaya kośa] is filled; *saḥ vai eṣaḥ,* that [vijñānamaya kośa]; *puruṣavidhaḥ eva,* has a human form; *tasya puruṣavidhatām anu ayam puruṣavidhaḥ,* in the way that [manomaya kośa] has a human form, in the same way this [vijñānamaya kośa] also has a human form; *tasya,* of that [vijñānamaya kośa]; *śraddhā,* respect for the scriptures; *eva śiraḥ,* is its head; *ṛtam,* thinking of the meaning of the scriptures; *dakṣiṇaḥ pakṣaḥ,* is its right wing; *satyam,* trying to mould one's speech and action according to the scriptures; *uttaraḥ pakṣaḥ,* is the left wing; *yogaḥ,* faultless practice of what the scriptures teach; *ātmā,* is the middle part of the body; *mahaḥ,* Hiraṇyagarbha [the first-born]; *puccham pratiṣṭhā,* is the supporting tail; *tat api eṣaḥ ślokaḥ bhavati,* there is a verse on this subject [in the brāhmaṇas]. *Iti caturthaḥ anuvākaḥ,* here ends the fourth chapter.

1. Words together with thoughts return from Brahman, unable to reach it. He who knows the bliss of Brahman is never afraid [of birth and death—i.e., he attains immortality].

This manomaya kośa is the self of the prāṇamaya kośa. There is yet another kośa known as the vijñānamaya kośa [the sheath of the intellect], which is inside the manomaya. The manomaya kośa is filled by the vijñānamaya kośa. The vijñānamaya kośa is also like a human body. Just as the manomaya kośa has a human form, in the same way the vijñānamaya kośa has a human form. *Śraddhā* [respect for the scriptures and for oneself] represents the head, *ṛta* [thinking of the meaning of the scriptures] represents its right wing, *satya* [truth] represents its left wing, and yoga represents its self, the middle part of the body. *Mahat,* or Hiraṇyagarbha, is the tail that gives support. There is a verse on this subject in the brāhmaṇas:

Both speech and mind fail to grasp or express the Supreme Brahman in the manomaya kośa. They have their limitations, but Brahman is limitless. Brahman is also too subtle for them. Furthermore, in no way can speech and mind be their own subject and object at the same time.

The word *vidvān* here means 'one who has experienced' —that is, experienced the supreme bliss of Self-knowledge. He is never afraid of anything. Why? Because there is nothing else. There is only the Self. What is there for him to fear? Fear arises only when there is more than one, but whatever exists is nothing but a manifestation of the Self.

Within the mental sheath, and separate from it, is the *vijñānamaya kośa,* the sheath of the intellect. It is called *ātmā,* the self, of the manomaya kośa, and also *śārīra,* because it occupies the *manomaya śarīra,* the mental body. The word *śārīra* is the adjective of *śarīra,* body. That which occupies the *śarīra* is the *śārīra.* Again, the vijñānamaya kośa is of the same form as the manomaya kośa. It is a replica, as it were.

Vijñānamaya is the level of the intellect. It is the level of decision, or determination. At the mental level there is always wavering and doubt—maybe yes, maybe no. But the intellect is firm. It decides: Yes, this.

The intellect also helps us understand the meaning of things. For instance, the Vedas tell us many things, but we have to be able to understand the real implication of what they say. Some people's minds work very superficially. They are not able to penetrate into the underlying meaning of the words.

There is a story about Indra, the king of the gods, and Virocana, the king of the demons. Both of them went to Prajāpati and asked: 'What is the Self? We hear about the Self, but what is it and where is it?' Prajāpati answered: 'Go to the river and look at your reflection. You will see the Self there.' Virocana went and looked at the reflection and saw his body. He thought, 'Oh, so the Self is the body.' He left, content with that knowledge. At first Indra also thought the Self was the body. But then he began to think: 'How can the Self be the body? The body changes. At one time it is young and at another time it is old. Sometimes it is sick and sometimes it is healthy. The Self is constant, without any change, so it cannot be the body.' After many years of questioning and meditating, he finally realized the real nature of the Self.

The Upaniṣad again gives the comparison with the parts of a bird. If the vijñānamaya kośa is thought of as a bird, what would its most important part, the head, be? The Upaniṣad says the head of the bird is *śraddhā,* which means faith in the scriptures and respect for them. It also means self-confidence. If you do not have self-confidence, you cannot make any decisions. And if you cannot make any decisions, you are lost. So you cannot afford to lose self-confidence.

Then *ṛtam,* righteousness, is the right wing of the bird. On the intellectual level, it means that you know what is right and you are conscious of your right decision. The left wing is *satyam,* truth. Truth means that there is harmony between your thought, speech, and action. Truth and righteousness—these two things are very important on the intellectual level. You don't expect an animal to be righteous or honest, but in the case of human beings, it is essential that they be so.

Then the body of the bird is said to be yoga. Śaṅkara says yoga means complete absorption, complete identification—*Yogaḥ yuktiḥ samādhānam.*

Self-knowledge is very subtle. How can you attain this knowledge? You can attain it when you have a combination of these three things—righteousness, truth, and complete absorption. When these are present you can utilize the intellect properly. Then the mind becomes purified and spiritual understanding develops.

Suppose you are very intelligent, but you are not righteous or honest. Recently there was a report of a bank robbery. The robbery was so well planned and organized, so well executed, that people had to admire the intelligence of the robbers. The police were completely stuck. They could not say who did it, as the robbers left no clue. A lot of money was taken, but there was no violence or bloodshed. So the Upaniṣad reminds us here that you may have intelligence, but you have to apply that intelligence in the right direction. Truth and righteousness are the two wings that will carry you forward.

Then the Upaniṣad says that the tail of the bird, the support, is *mahaḥ. Mahaḥ* means *mahattattvam,* or Hiraṇyagarbha, the first manifestation of Brahman. Śaṅkara says: *Kāraṇaṁ hi kāryāṇāṁ pratiṣṭhā*—the cause is the support (*pratiṣṭhā*) of the effect. That is to say, there can be no effect without a cause. So also, this vijñānamaya kośa cannot function and develop without *mahaḥ.* Śaṅkara compares it to the trees and creepers on the earth (*yathā vṛkṣavīrudhāṁ pṛthivī*). The earth is the support of the trees and creepers, and without the earth there could not be any trees or creepers. Similarly, Hiraṇyagarbha is the support of everything.

Chapter Five

विज्ञानं यज्ञं तनुते। कर्माणि तनुतेऽपि च। विज्ञानं देवाः सर्वे। ब्रह्म ज्येष्ठमुपासते। विज्ञानं ब्रह्म चेद्वेद। तस्माच्चेन्न प्रमाद्यति। शरीरे पाप्मनो हित्वा। सर्वान्कामा-न्समश्नुत इति।

तस्यैष एव शारीर आत्मा। यः पूर्वस्य। तस्माद्वा एतस्माद्विज्ञानमयात्। अन्योऽन्तर आत्माऽऽनन्दमयः। तेनैष पूर्णः। स वा एष पुरुषविध एव। तस्य पुरुषविधताम्। अन्वयं पुरुषविधः। तस्य प्रियमेव शिरः। मोदो दक्षिणः पक्षः। प्रमोद उत्तरः पक्षः। आनन्द आत्मा। ब्रह्म पुच्छं प्रतिष्ठा। तदप्येष श्लोको भवति॥ १॥ इति पञ्चमोऽनुवाकः॥

Vijñānaṁ yajñaṁ tanute; Karmāṇi tanute'pi ca; Vijñānaṁ devāḥ sarve; Brahma jyeṣṭhamupāsate; Vijñānaṁ brahma cedveda; Tasmāccenna pramādyati; Śarīre pāpmano hitvā; Sarvānkāmānsamaśnuta iti.

Tasyaiṣa eva śārīra ātmā; Yaḥ pūrvasya; Tasmādvā etasmādvijñānamayāt; Anyo'ntara ātmā''nandamayaḥ; Tenaiṣa pūrṇaḥ; Sa vā eṣa puruṣavidha eva; Tasya puruṣavidhatām; Anvayaṁ puruṣavidhaḥ; Tasya priyameva śiraḥ; Modo dakṣiṇaḥ pakṣaḥ; Pramoda uttaraḥ pakṣaḥ; Ānanda ātmā; Brahma pucchaṁ pratiṣṭhā; Tadapyeṣa śloko bhavati. Iti pañcamo'nuvākaḥ.

Vijñānam, the intellect as the self; *yajñam,* ceremonies such as the Agnihotra; *tanute,* perform; *karmāni,* normal activities; *api ca tanute,* also continue doing; *sarve devāḥ,* all the sense organs [or their presiding deities]; *jyeṣṭham,* the first-born; *vijñānam brahma,* Brahman seen as the intellect; *upāsate,* meditate on; *cet,* if; *vijñānam brahma veda,* a person knows the intellect as Brahman; *cet,* [and] if; *tasmāt,* from that [i.e., from treating the intellect as Brahman]; *na pramādyati,* he never deviates; *śarīre pāpmanaḥ hitvā,* having renounced any thought of the body being his identity [and the errors that follow from that kind of thought]; *sarvān kāmān samaśnute iti,* he enjoys everything he desires.

Tasya pūrvasya yaḥ eṣaḥ eva śārīraḥ ātmā, this [vijñānamaya kośa] is the indwelling self of the aforesaid [manomaya kośa]; *tasmāt vai etasmāt vijñānamayāt anyaḥ antaraḥ ātmā,* deeper within this vijñānamaya kośa is another self; *ānandamayaḥ,* [called] the ānandamaya kośa [the sheath of bliss]; *tena eṣaḥ pūrṇaḥ,* by that [ānandamaya kośa] this [vijñānamaya kośa] is filled; *saḥ vai eṣaḥ,* that [ānandamaya kośa]; *puruṣavidhaḥ eva,* has a human form; *tasya puruṣa-vidhatām anu ayam puruṣavidhaḥ,* in the way that [i.e., the vijñānamaya kośa] has a human form, in the same way this [ānandamaya kośa] also has a human form; *tasya,* of that [ānandamaya kośa]; *priyam,* happiness [for instance, from seeing something one likes]; *eva śiraḥ,* is the head; *modaḥ,* pleasure [from getting something one loves]; *dakṣiṇaḥ pakṣaḥ,* is the right wing; *pramodaḥ,* the pleasure of enjoying things [for instance, eating something one likes]; *uttaraḥ pakṣaḥ,* is the left wing; *ānandaḥ ātmā,* bliss is the self [the middle part of the body]; *brahma puccham pratiṣṭhā,* Brahman [one without a second] is the tail that supports; *tat api eṣaḥ ślokaḥ bhavati,* there is a verse about this. *Iti pañcamaḥ anuvākaḥ,* here ends the fifth chapter.

1. An intelligent person goes on performing sacrifices with great respect and also promotes all kinds of activities. [And, because of his intelligence, he is able to discriminate between what is good work and what is not.] Aware of the importance of intelligence, Indra and the rest of the gods and goddesses worship Brahman, who is the chief of all intelligent beings. A person may have many blemishes due to his association with a body, but if he knows Brahman and never stops thinking of him, he will nevertheless get rid of those blemishes. He will also enjoy everything he wants. This is the vijñānamaya self, Brahman as intelligence. It is the embodied self of the aforesaid manomaya self.

Within the vijñānamaya kośa [the self as intelligence] there is another self known as the ānandamaya kośa [the self as bliss]. The vijñānamaya kośa is filled by the ānandamaya kośa. The ānandamaya kośa is also like a human body. Just as the vijñānamaya kośa has a human form, in the same way the ānandamaya kośa has a human form. The joy of seeing things you like is the head, the joy of acquiring things you like is the right wing, the joy of enjoying things you like is the left wing, and bliss is the self [the middle part of the body]. Brahman, one without a second, is the supporting tail. There is a verse [in the brāhmaṇas] about this:

Vijñānam yajñam tanute. Vijñānam means the *buddhi,* the intellect, the determinative faculty. *Tanute* means 'it performs.' Through your intellect you perform many sacrifices, and you also perform your duties. Everything is decided by the intellect. An animal is driven by instinct. It does not know what is good or bad, what is right or wrong. But a human being can use his intellect to decide what his duties are and what he should and should not do.

Perhaps all of us worship a person who has a fine intellect. The Upaniṣad says that even the gods worship the intellect. There are people who are always carried away by their emotions, or even by their instincts. They do not stop to think about what they are doing. But a person who uses his judgement never makes a mistake. The intellect is our guide, so it is to be revered. It is also said to be the first born (*jyeṣṭham*). Just as we revere that person who is the oldest, so also we revere the intellect, which is the first born. This is all in praise of the intellect. The Upanisad, you may notice, is giving the maximum importance to the intellect.

Why should you worship your intellect as Brahman? Because then you will never deviate from what it tells you to do. And, the Upaniṣad says, if you follow your intellect, you will overcome all your weaknesses and limitations. You will no longer be a slave to your body. As you may know, Saint Francis used to call the body 'Brother Ass.' An ass has very little brains. It cannot guide itself; it has to be guided. So also, our bodies have to be guided by our intellect so that we do not make mistakes. The Upaniṣad is telling us to transcend the gross physical level and go to the subtle level. We should not be so occupied with the physical body. Very often it is when we attach too much importance to our body that we behave foolishly.

Then why does the Upaniṣad say that if you worship the intellect you can enjoy all your desires? The Upaniṣad says that when you are pursuing something on the intellectual level—provided, of course, it is something good—you become very happy. But if you are driven by emotions and passions, you will naturally make many mistakes, and then there is no question of your being happy. If you can steadfastly follow your goal without being swayed by physical cravings and emotions, you enjoy life much more.

Then the Upaniṣad discusses the *ānandamaya kośa,* the sheath of bliss. The same idea is given here as in previous verses, that it is separate from the vijñānamaya kośa, and of the same form as the body.

Now if the sheath of bliss is thought of as a bird, what would the head of this bird be? *Priya,* joy. Śaṅkara explains it as the kind of experience you have when you see a loved one. For instance, to parents, seeing their children brings the greatest joy. Suppose your son has gone abroad and has been away for several years. On a certain day he is expected to return. You are anxiously waiting for him, and finally you see him. *Priya* is that kind of joy.

Moda is the right wing. Śaṅkara says it is the kind of joy you feel when you get something you have always wanted. Suppose you have been trying to buy a car for many years. You have been saving your money and just waiting for the day when you have enough. Finally one day you are able to buy it. That kind of happiness is *moda.* The left wing of the bird is *pramoda.* Śaṅkara does not give any example of this, but he says *pramoda* means *prakṛṣṭaḥ harṣaḥ,* immense joy.

This ānandamaya kośa is not the real Self. At that level we are close to the Self, but there is still a barrier. Just as the nearer you go to the Himalayas the colder you feel, so also, the nearer you approach the Self, the more joy you feel. Ānanda, or bliss, is said to be the self—that is, the trunk—of the bird. It is because of the real Self, that the individual self and everything connected with it become dear. The bliss you have when you know your Self is real and permanent, and you know your Self when you have a pure mind, a mind free from all desires.

According to Śaṅkara, when you enjoy worldly things

you may get joy, but this kind of joy is temporary. He says: Suppose the cause for your joy is not there. What happens then? For instance, suppose the son you were waiting for does not come. Where is your joy then? Or suppose the car that you bought after so much trouble is destroyed in an accident. Then there is only unhappiness.

But spiritual joy does not depend on any external factor. With spiritual joy you are happy in spite of external conditions, not because of them. Even when Sri Ramakrishna was suffering from throat cancer, his face was beaming with joy. He radiated joy.

But where does all this joy come from? From Brahman. So Brahman, or the Self, is said to be the *puccham,* the tail, or support. The Self is the source of all joys, and that is why the joy you get from the Self is always there. And because of the presence of the Self, other things also give us joy. Why do cars or food or children give us joy? Because they are all manifestations of Brahman. All things rest on ānanda. They are expressions of ānanda, of Brahman. When you know your children are Brahman, you get another kind of joy. You get more joy.

But the highest joy comes when you know you are one with that Brahman. Śaṅkara says that this Brahman is the *ābhyantaram,* the inmost Self. Because of him we exist. Because we see duality, we suffer. But in Brahman all dualities end. You become one with that joy that is Brahman.

Chapter Six

असन्नेव स भवति। असद्ब्रह्मेति वेद चेत्। अस्ति ब्रह्मेति चेद्वेद। सन्तमेनं ततो विदुरिति।

तस्यैष एव शारीर आत्मा। यः पूर्वस्य। अथातोऽनुप्रश्नाः। उताविद्वानमुं लोकं प्रेत्य कश्चन गच्छती ३। आहो विद्वानमुं लोकं प्रेत्य कश्चित्समश्नुता ३ उ।

सोऽकामयत। बहु स्यां प्रजायेयेति। स तपोऽतप्यत। स तपस्तप्त्वा। इद सर्वमसृजत। यदिदं किंच। तत्सृष्ट्वा तदेवानुप्राविशत्। तदनुप्रविश्य। सच्च त्यच्चाभवत्। निरुक्तं चानिरुक्तं च। निलयनं चानिलयनं च। विज्ञानं चाविज्ञानं च। सत्यं चानृतं च सत्यमभवत्। यदिदं किंच। तत्सत्यमित्याचक्षते तदप्येष श्लोको भवति॥ १॥ इति षष्ठोऽनुवाकः॥

Asanneva sa bhavati; Asadbrahmeti veda cet; Asti brahmeti cedveda; Santamenaṁ tato viduriti.

Tasyaiṣa eva śārīra ātmā; Yaḥ pūrvasya; Athāto-'nupraśnāḥ; Utāvidvānamuṁ lokaṁ pretya kaścana gacchatī 3; Āho vidvānamuṁ lokaṁ pretya kaścitsam-aśnutā 3 u.

So'kāmayata; Bahu syāṁ prajāyeyeti; Sa tapo'tapya-

ta; Sa tapastaptvā; Idaṁ sarvamasṛjata; Yadidaṁ kiṁca; Tatsṛṣṭvā tadevānuprāviśat; Tadanupraviśya; Sacca tyaccābhavat; Niruktaṁ cāniruktaṁ ca; Nilayanaṁ cānilayanaṁ ca; Vijñānaṁ cāvijñānaṁ ca; Satyaṁ cānṛtaṁ ca satyamabhavat; Yadidaṁ kiṁca; Tatsatyam-ityācakṣate tadapyeṣa śloko bhavati. Iti ṣaṣṭho'nuvākaḥ.

Cet, if; *brahma asat iti veda,* [a person] knows that Brahman does not exist; *saḥ asan eva bhavati,* he himself becomes non-existent; *brahma asti,* Brahman exists; *iti cet veda,* if anyone knows; *tataḥ,* in that case; [*brahmavidaḥ,* those who know Brahman]; *enam santam viduh iti,* know him to be real.

Yaḥ, that [ānandamaya self, the sheath of bliss]; *esah eva tasya pūrvasya śārīraḥ ātmā,* embodied in the aforesaid [vijñānamaya self]; *ataḥ,* therefore; *atha,* after [the disciples had completed their studies]; *anu,* in the wake of [what the teacher had said]; *praśnāḥ,* [these] questions [may be raised]; *kaścana avidvān,* does any ignorant person [i.e., ignorant of the Self]; *pretya,* after death; *amum lokam,* that world [the Cosmic Self]; *gacchati,* attain; *3,* or does he not; *uta āho kaścit vidvān,* or does one who knows the Self; *pretya,* after death; *amum lokam,* that Cosmic Self; *samaśnutā,* attain; *3,* or does he not?

Saḥ, he [the Cosmic Self]; *akāmayata,* wished [thought within himself]; *bahu syām prajāyeya iti,* I will be born as many; [next,] *saḥ,* he [the Cosmic Self]; *tapaḥ atapyata,* thought and decided; *saḥ tapaḥ taptvā,* he, having so decided; *idam sarvam asṛjata,* created all that exists; *idam,* this [the living and the non-living]; *yat kiṁca,* whatever there is; *tat,* this world [with living and non-living things]; *sṛṣṭvā,* having created; *tat eva anuprāviśat,* he entered into it all; *tat anupraviśya sat abhavat,* having entered, he assumed forms; *tyat ca,* and also became formless; *niruktam ca aniruktam ca,* with well-defined [time and space] and without; *nilayanam ca anilayanam ca,* with a resting place and without it; *vijñānam ca avijñānam ca,* the conscious and the unconscious; *satyam ca anṛtam ca,* empirically true or its opposite; *satyam abhavat,* [because] that Truth [i.e., Brahman] manifested itself; *yat idam kiṁca,* [as] whatever there is [around us]; *tat satyam iti ācakṣate,* [the knowers of Brahman] refer to it [i.e., Brahman] as Truth; *tat api eṣaḥ ślokaḥ bhavati,* there is also a verse in this connection. *Iti ṣaṣṭhaḥ anuvākaḥ,* here ends the sixth chapter.

1. If anyone knows that Brahman does not exist, then he himself becomes non-existent. [Again,] if anyone knows that Brahman exists, then those who know Brahman will regard him as Brahman.

This [ānandamaya self, the self as bliss] is the embodied self of the aforesaid [vijñānamaya kośa, the sheath of intelligence]. In the wake of what the teacher had said, the disciple might ask: 'Does a person ignorant of the Self attain Self-knowledge after death, or does he not? Does a person who knows the Self attain Self-knowledge after death, or does he not?'

The Cosmic Self thought to himself: 'I will become many. I will be born.' He then practised austerities. In his case, he only thought. Then he created the whole world of living and non-living things. He created them and then entered into them. Having entered into them, he in some cases assumed forms and in other cases remained formless. In some cases he was characterized by distinct time and place, and in other cases time and place were not distinct. In some cases he had a shelter [he needed it], and in other cases he had none [he needed none—because he was formless]. Also, in some cases he was conscious and in other cases unconscious. Brahman, the Truth, also manifested itself as relative truth, as untruth, and so on. Because Brahman manifested itself as all things around us, those who know Brahman call it 'Truth.' There is a verse in this connection:

Cet means 'if.' If someone says that Brahman does not exist, then, the Upaniṣad says, he is denying his own existence. And it is as if he himself becomes non-existent. Many people say: 'There is no such thing as Brahman. It is all nonsense. We do not see Brahman, so how can we say it exists?' Many people think that the only existence is what they can experience through the senses. But why does the Upaniṣad say that such a person becomes non-existent? Because Brahman is your own Self. Can you deny your own existence? It is as if you are saying, 'I do not exist.'

Now you may protest: 'I am not saying *I* do not exist. I am saying *Brahman* does not exist. I am something separate.' But the Upaniṣad says that you *are* Brahman. The Upaniṣad is here equating Brahman with the Self.

But suppose a person says that he knows Brahman exists. He is convinced. He speaks with authority. Then, by virtue of that knowledge, people know that he has become one with Brahman, that he has had a direct, personal experience of Brahman. The word *tataḥ* is very significant. It means 'from that'—that is, from the fact that he has had this experience of Brahman, or by virtue of that knowledge. Now many people say, 'Brahman exists,' or 'God exists,' but for them it is merely an intellectual assertion. We must have firsthand knowledge. We must have a direct, personal experience. Then our knowledge is valid.

When Swami Vivekananda first came to Sri Ramakrishna, he asked: 'Sir, have you seen God?' He had previously asked many people this question, but most people had given an evasive answer. But Sri Ramakrishna immediately replied: 'Yes, I have seen God. In fact, I see him more clearly than I see you. And if you so desire I can show him to you.' When a person like Sri Ramakrishna says this, you are forced to accept his testimony. His words have authority.

Now some questions (*anupraśnāḥ*) arise. *Praśna* means 'question,' and *anu* means 'following,' or 'arising from.' So far, the teacher has been instructing the students. But now the students want some clarification. The first question concerns an ignorant person. *Avidvān* means here a person who has not attained Self-knowledge. In *The Gospel of Sri Ramakrishna,* when M. (Master Mahashay) first came to Sri Ramakrishna, he mentioned that his wife was an ignorant person. At once Sri Ramakrishna said sharply: 'What! And you are a man of knowledge?' M. thought that because he had a college degree he was very learned. But Sri Ramakrishna pointed out that there was another kind of knowledge, and that knowledge of the Self is real knowledge. All other knowledge is just another form of ignorance.

Here the students want to know what happens when a person who has not realized Brahman dies. Does he enter into Brahman, the world of bliss? Lots of people think that the body is the stumbling block. They think the body is responsible for their bondage, and if they can just throw it off, they will be free. Many people commit suicide thinking that they will at once become free. But Vedānta says no, you will not become free merely by destroying the body. You will still be in bondage. Why? Because of your ignorance (*avidyā*), ignorance of your own Self. Because of your ignorance, you are born again and again. You are caught in the cycle of birth and death. Only when you know your Self will you become free.

You may have noticed the number 3 in the text. This sign is called *pluti.* It means the converse. The question is, 'Does he attain Brahman?' And the 3 means, 'Or does he not?'

Now, apparently what is being asked is: Do we need knowledge in order to attain the world of Brahman? But the real import of the question is: If Brahman is impartial, like the sun, or like space, then why do you say that we can only reach Brahman through knowledge? Whether we are wise or ignorant, what difference does it make? After death we should all be equal. There is an English poem that refers to death as 'the leveller.' All become one—king or peasant, ruler or ruled. All become levelled down to the same state. So whether I am ignorant or have knowledge, it is all the same so far as Brahman is concerned. Therefore, why shouldn't we all go to Brahman then? So the implication is, either Brahman is partial, or else Brahman does not exist and no one attains Brahman.

The idea in Vedānta, however, is that you are always Brahman, whether you know it or not. Sri Ramakrishna gives the example of a stick placed across a pond. The stick seems to divide the pond in two, but in reality the water is never divided. Similarly, because of our names and forms we seem to be separate individuals, and separate from Brahman. But when we realize our true nature, when we cease to identify ourselves with our names and forms, we know that we were never separate from Brahman.

Śaṅkara raises here the issue about the existence of Brahman. Suppose someone argues: Anything that exists, such as a pot, can be seen or felt. It is an object of perception. And anything that does not exist, such as the horns of a rabbit, we can never see or feel. Does anyone see or feel Brahman? How then can you say Brahman exists?

Śaṅkara answers: Whatever we see in this universe, starting from the finest element, *ākāśa* (space), has a cause. There are two categories: cause (*kāraṇa*) and effect (*kārya*). Something may be the cause of an effect, but yet it may also be the effect of some other cause. For instance, earth is the cause of an earthen pot, yet earth is also the effect of another cause. Earth has been derived from other elements, so it is an effect, yet in relation to the pot it is the cause.

If you go on like this you find yourself following a chain of cause and effect, cause and effect, one after another, until you come to the finest element, *ākāśa,* space. But, as an element, *ākāśa* also must have come out of something.

Śaṅkara says, could all this existence have come out of non-existence? Can something come out of nothing? Finally you have to accept that there is a first cause, and that first cause is called Brahman. It is the source of everything. Brahman is the ultimate from which everything has been derived.

Srī Ramakrishna used to give the example of the number one. If you put a zero after it, it becomes ten. If you put another zero, it becomes a hundred, and so on. But if you take away the one, you have nothing but zeros. Brahman is like that number one. Everything exists because Brahman exists. Brahman is the source of all existence.

Now the Upaniṣad says that Brahman had a desire (*saḥ akāmayata*): *'Bahu syām*—I will become many.' Does that mean Brahman is a mortal like us? We have desires. We desire wealth or power or health or social status. Sometimes our desires are good and sometimes they are not, but we always have a sense of want or discontent within us. So why should we want to attain Brahman if Brahman is like us?

Śaṅkara says, no, Brahman is independent (*svatantra*). He is his own master. When we have desires, we are completely at the mercy of those desires, and we are dependent on so many things. We are slaves to our desires and slaves to other people, so when we do something we are compelled to do it. But Brahman is under no compulsion to act.

The next question is, how did Brahman become many? Śaṅkara says Brahman does not produce something outside himself. That which is within himself he manifests. The names and forms are within him, and these are projected out, so we think we are separate from Brahman and separate from each other. In essence we are all one, but we are separate in terms of names and forms. Men, women, animals, plants—all are the same Brahman. But we do not see Brahman. We see only names and forms.

So the Upaniṣad says Brahman just thought. Here the word *tapaḥ* means knowledge. It was merely his thought, or wish. Usually *tapaḥ* means austerity. If we want to make something, we have to work very hard and we have to have different tools. But Brahman just contemplated, and then this universe came into being. Brahman is like a seed. Out of a seed a tree comes. Does the seed have to work hard to bring out the tree? No, it happens naturally. In the same way, Brahman brings out this universe—the whole universe, whatever exists. We see only a part of this universe. There is much of it that we cannot see. But whatever is there, seen or unseen, with form or without form, comes from Brahman.

Then the Upaniṣad says that after projecting this universe, Brahman entered into it. *Anuprāviśat* means 'he entered.' This part of the text is very controversial, and Śaṅkara is at great pains to explain this word. How did Brahman enter? One objection is: Suppose you are a potter and you make a pot. Can you enter into the pot after you make it?

Or, another objection is: This idea of entering suggests that Brahman has a form. Who enters? Someone who has a form. There is a house and then someone enters it. So the house is one thing and the person is another. Or, maybe it is like my hand entering into my mouth. I am one individual body, but a part of this body, my hand, goes inside another, my mouth.

Śaṅkara says no, it is like this: Suppose there is a pot in a room, but the room is dark so you cannot see it. If you bring a lamp then you can see the pot. The pot was there all the time, only the darkness kept you from seeing it. Similarly, Brahman is everywhere—within you, within me, within everyone. We cannot see it because of ignorance. But when we attain knowledge it *seems* as if Brahman has entered inside us, though it is always there. Knowledge is that light and our ignorance is the darkness.

Chapter Seven

असद्वा इदमग्र आसीत्। ततो वै सदजायत।
तदात्मानꣳ स्वयमकुरुत। तस्मात्तत्सुकृतमुच्यत इति।

यद्वै तत् सुकृतम्। रसो वै सः। रसꣳ ह्येवायं लब्ध्वाऽऽनन्दी भवति। को ह्येवान्यात्कः प्राण्यात्। यदेष आकाश आनन्दो न स्यात्। एष ह्येवाऽऽनन्दयाति। यदा ह्येवैष एतस्मिन्नदृश्येऽनात्म्येऽनिरुक्तेऽनिलयनेऽभयं प्रतिष्ठां विन्दते। अथ सोऽभयं गतो भवति। यदा ह्येवैष एतस्मिन्नुदरमन्तरं कुरुते। अथ तस्य भयं भवति। तत्त्वेव भयं विदुषोऽमन्वानस्य। तदप्येष श्लोको भवति॥ १॥ इति सप्तमोऽनुवाकः॥

Asadvā idamagra āsīt; Tato vai sadajāyata; Tadātmānaṁ svayamakuruta; Tasmāttatsukṛtamucyata iti.

Yadvai tat sukṛtam; Raso vai saḥ; Rasaṁ hyevāyaṁ labdhvā''nandī bhavati; Ko hyevānyātkaḥ prāṇyāt; Yadeṣa ākāśa ānando na syāt; Eṣa hyevā''nandayāti; Yadā hyevaiṣa etasminnadṛśye'nātmye'nirukte'nilayane'bhayaṁ pratiṣṭhāṁ vindate; Atha so'bhayaṁ gato bhavati; Yadā hyevaiṣa etasminnudaramantaraṁ kurute; Atha tasya bhayaṁ bhavati; Tattveva bhayaṁ viduṣo'manvānasya; Tadapyeṣa śloko bhavati. Iti saptamo'nuvākaḥ.

Idam, this [phenomenal world]; *agre,* originally; *asat vai āsīt,* was non-existent [i.e., it was, in fact, unmanifested Brahman]; *tataḥ vai,* from that [unmanifested state]; *sat,* this world with its diverse names and forms; *ajāyata,* emerged; *tat,* that [Brahman]; *svayam ātmānam akuruta,* manifested himself; *tasmāt,* this is why; *tat,* that [Brahman]; *sukṛtam,* 'a good creator' or, 'the self-created'; *ucyate iti,* is called [by the sages].

Yat tat vai sukṛtam, that which is 'sukṛta'; *saḥ,* that; *rasaḥ vai,* is to be identified as the sweetness [in everything]; *ayam hi rasam eva labdhvā,* anyone who has this sweetness [knows the Self, the source of sweetness]; *ānandī bhavati,* is happy; *ākāśe,* in the space inside the heart; *eṣaḥ,* this [Self]; *yat ānandaḥ na syāt,* if [it] were not the source of happiness; [then] *kaḥ hi eva anyāt,* who would care even to breathe; *kaḥ prāṇyāt,* who would care to live; *hi,* therefore; *eṣaḥ,* this [Self inside the heart]; *eva anandayāti,* gives happiness [to all]; *eṣaḥ,* this [Self]; *eva hi yadā,* when; *adṛśye,* becomes invisible; *anātmye,* leaves the body [and, for that reason]; *anirukte,* it cannot be described; *anilayane,* not resting on anything [i.e., free from all modifications]; *etasmin,* in this [Self]; *abhayam,* without fear [such as from being born again]; *pratiṣṭhām,* resting in one's own Self; *vindate,* attains; *atha,* thereafter; *saḥ,* the person [who has attained this state]; *abhayam gataḥ bhavati,* has no fear [of being born again]; [on the other hand] *eṣaḥ,* this [person]; *eva yadā,* if [the same person]; *etasmin,* in this [Self]; *ut aram,* even a little; *antaram,* separateness; *kurute,* does [i.e., discriminates]; *atha,* because of [this sense of separateness]; *tasya,* the person [who makes this discrimination]; *bhayam bhavati,* he is frightened; *tu,* but; *amanvānasya,* of that foolish person; *viduṣaḥ,* the person who thinks he is separate from the Self; *tat eva,* that [Brahman] again; *bhayam,* [is a cause of] fear; *tat api eṣaḥ ślokaḥ bhavati,* there is a verse on this subject. *Iti saptamaḥ anuvākaḥ,* here ends the seventh chapter.

1. At first there was no world. There was only Brahman. The world was then in Brahman, who was unmanifested. The world, with all its names and forms, then manifested itself. It was as if Brahman created himself this way. Because Brahman created himself, he came to be known as *Sukṛta* [i.e., 'Well-created,' or 'Self-created'].

As Sukṛta, he is also bliss. When a person attains bliss, he is happy. The Self within each of us is the source of our bliss. If it were not so, who would care to live, or even to breathe? The Self is beyond the reach of the sense organs. It is independent and without any attributes. When a person rests fearlessly in that Self, he is no longer afraid of anything. So long as he sees the least difference between himself and the Cosmic Self, he is not altogether free from fear. A person may be learned, but if he still thinks he is separate from Brahman, Brahman itself becomes a source of terror [though it is supposed to take one beyond fear]. There is a verse on this subject:

In this verse we come across two words that have special meanings—*sat* and *asat.* Literally, *sat* means 'that which exists.' In that sense, Brahman alone is *sat.* It always exists, under all circumstances. Everything else then is *asat,* non-existent, or ephemeral, because everything other than Brahman exists only for a certain time and under certain circumstances. But here the word *sat* means that which is manifest, or seen. It refers to this phenomenal world. It is Brahman manifested as this universe. And the word *asat* means that which is unmanifest, which is not seen. It is Brahman as the source of everything.

Suppose there is a huge banyan tree before us. There are so many branches and leaves on this tree. Where did it come from? From a seed. It was within the seed, but it was then unmanifest. You cannot say it did not exist. Similarly, at first this universe was in an unmanifested state (*asat*). It was within Brahman in a seed form. Now it has become manifested (*sat*).

Idam—this. *Tataḥ*—from that. You notice, the Upaniṣad doesn't use the word Brahman here. We find these words, *idam* and *tat,* used again and again in Vedānta. *Idam* refers to this physical universe, which is present before us. We are very much conscious of this *idam,* this universe. But when we say *tat,* that, it suggests something that is not right before us, something we can't see. So the Upaniṣad is saying *this* universe has come out of *that* Brahman, which we do not see.

But if Brahman created this universe, who created him? The Upaniṣad says he has no creator. He created himself (*svayam akuruta*). That is to say, he manifested himself. You notice, there is no duality here. He is the creator as well as the creation. That is, when he is manifested there is the creation. This answers the objection brought up in the previous verse about Brahman entering into his creation. Here the Upaniṣad says that the creator and the creation are the same. *Sukṛtam* has two meanings. *Su-kṛtam* could mean good or well done. Or the word may mean *sva-kṛtam,* self-created, created by himself.

Rasaḥ vai saḥ—Brahman is *rasa,* bliss. He is the source of all joy. The idea is that even physical joy is derived from Brahman. It is being filtered through the senses. If we get good food, that is joy filtered through the tongue. All of us get joy in some form or another. The Upaniṣads do not say that this universe is only suffering. No one is completely lost. Maybe your concept of joy and another person's concept of joy are different. You may get joy from reading good poetry, and someone else may get joy from eating good food or wearing good clothes. But whatever joy you get comes from one source—Brahman.

If you have a pet dog, you may have noticed that it feels very happy when you are around. The fact that your dog feels this happiness proves that Brahman is within it. It also derives its happiness from the same source, Brahman. Those who know Brahman know that this joy is within them. It does not come from outside.

Why do we work so hard for money? Why do we run after good food or good books? Because we think they will give us joy. We are always searching for joy. That is the one thing we are struggling for. Who would care to live if there were not some joy in life? Suppose there were no joy; there was only hardship and suffering. Life would be impossible. The Upaniṣad says we would not even care to breathe. But we can always find some joy, whether physical, intellectual, or spiritual because Brahman, the source of joy, is within us, in our heart.

But this is not to deny suffering. Suffering is in the very nature of life. In some cases our suffering is compensated by some joy, yet we often have to pay dearly for the joy we get. At times it seems there is more suffering than joy in life. When we suffer we think: 'I have never known happiness in my life. I have always suffered. I live a cursed life.' But then, when we get some happiness, we are so taken up by it that we forget about our suffering altogether.

If Brahman is the source of joy, then where does our pain and suffering come from? Our suffering comes from our ignorance. When we know Brahman we no longer have any more suffering. We attain pure, unalloyed happiness, happiness that never ends.

Brahman is described here as *adṛśya,* invisible. It cannot be seen. And it is *anātmā,* without a form. Here, *ātmā* does not mean the soul. It means a form. Because Brahman is without a form, you cannot see it. Then again, it is *anirukta,* beyond speech. You cannot describe it or talk about it. How many things can we describe through words? Very often we cannot even describe our own feelings. We keep quiet. When the heart is full we are silent. Then the Upaniṣad says Brahman is *anilayanam,* without any resting place or abode. You cannot say that Brahman is here or there or anywhere. Brahman is everywhere.

What happens to you when you know Brahman? You attain the state of fearlessness. *Abhayam,* fearlessness—that is your real state. That is Brahman. Brahman is the *pratiṣṭhām,* the ground, the support. And that Brahman is your own Self. Can you be afraid of your own Self?

The word *pratiṣṭhā* also has the connotation of being self-contained, sovereign, or independent. That is, you don't depend on anyone. When you have to depend on other people or on certain circumstances, you are always insecure. For instance, if you are a farmer you have to depend on the whims of nature. You may not get any rain or it may rain too much and your crops are destroyed. So fear and apprehension are always there. We are constantly searching for a state in which we can feel we are our own master, where external forces cannot keep us bound. That is why we dare to challenge nature. We dare the impossible. Why do we land a spaceship on the moon? It is the call of the infinite. It is the call of the human spirit, and that spirit is Brahman. It is our own Self.

The Upaniṣad says that if you have even a little (*ut aram*) of this idea that you are separate from Brahman then you are ignorant, then you have fear. You may say: 'Well, I am trying to attain Self-knowledge, but I have not yet attained it. I am very close to Brahman, but I am not yet Brahman.' This is absurd. Either you are Brahman or you are not Brahman. It is a question of knowledge, of conviction. If you know you are Brahman, nothing can shake you from that position. Nothing can make you afraid.

Śaṅkara says that seeing many is ignorance and is the cause of our fear. If there is duality—two elements or two beings—then there is room for conflict, clash, or competition. Then there is fear. But when a person realizes that he is the one Self, then he sees no second being, he hears no second being, he knows no second being. There is only 'I'. If there is consciousness of 'you' and 'I', that means there is a separation. That means there is ignorance. But when you are conscious that the same Self is everywhere—that you are everywhere—only in different forms and under different names, then the question of fear does not arise.

Śaṅkara compares this ignorance to someone who has defective eyesight and sees two moons in the sky. Are there two moons in the sky? No, of course not. Just because someone sees two moons does not make it a fact. Similarly, an ignorant person sees many, but that does not make it real.

Śaṅkara says, such a person laments: *'Īśvaraḥ anyaḥ mattaḥ aham anyaḥ saṁsārī*—God is separate from me. I am a worldly person, a sinner, different from him.' Swami Vivekananda used to say that the greatest sin was to think of yourself as a sinner. God is always within us—here, in our heart. If he is within, then he cannot be separate from us. He is within and also without, immanent as well as transcendent. Brahman is everywhere.

Chapter Eight

भीषाऽस्माद्वातः पवते। भीषोदेति सूर्यः। भीषाऽस्मादग्निश्चेन्द्रश्च। मृत्युर्धावति पञ्चम इति। सैषाऽऽनन्दस्य मीमाꣳसा भवति। युवा स्यात्साधुयुवाऽध्यायकः। आशिष्ठो दृढिष्ठो बलिष्ठः। तस्येयं पृथिवी सर्वा वित्तस्य पूर्णा स्यात्। स एको मानुष आनन्दः। ते ये शतं मानुषा आनन्दाः ॥ १ ॥

स एको मनुष्यगन्धर्वाणामानन्दः। श्रोत्रियस्य चाकामहतस्य। ते ये शतं मनुष्यगन्धर्वाणामानन्दाः। स एको देवगन्धर्वाणामानन्दः। श्रोत्रियस्य चाकामहतस्य। ते ये शतं देवगन्धर्वाणामानन्दाः। स एकः पितृणां चिरलोकलोकानामानन्दः। श्रोत्रियस्य चाकामहतस्य। ते ये शतं पितृणां चिरलोकलोकानामानन्दाः। स एक आजानजानां देवानामानन्दः ॥ २ ॥

श्रोत्रियस्य चाकामहतस्य। ते ये शतमाजानजानां देवानामानन्दाः। स एकः कर्मदेवानां देवानामानन्दः। ये

कर्मणा देवानपियन्ति। श्रोत्रियस्य चाकामहतस्य। ते ये शतं कर्मदेवानां देवानामानन्दाः। स एको देवानामानन्दः। श्रोत्रियस्य चाकामहतस्य। ते ये शतं देवानामानन्दाः। स एक इन्द्रस्याऽऽनन्दः॥ ३॥

श्रोत्रियस्य चाकामहतस्य। ते ये शतमिन्द्रस्याऽऽनन्दाः। स एको बृहस्पतेरानन्दः। श्रोत्रियस्य चाकामहतस्य। ते ये शतं बृहस्पतेरानन्दाः। स एकः प्रजापतेरानन्दः। श्रोत्रियस्य चाकामहतस्य। ते ये शतं प्रजापतेरानन्दाः। स एको ब्रह्मण आनन्दः। श्रोत्रियस्य चाकामहतस्य॥ ४॥

Bhīṣā'smādvātaḥ pavate; Bhīṣodeti sūryaḥ; Bhīṣā-'smādagniścendraśca; Mṛtyurdhāvati pañcama iti; Saiṣā-''nandasya mīmāṁsā bhavati; Yuvā syātsādhuyuvā-'dhyāyakaḥ; Āśiṣṭho dṛḍhiṣṭho baliṣṭhaḥ; Tasyeyaṁ pṛthivī sarvā vittasya pūrṇā syāt; Sa eko mānuṣa ānandaḥ; Te ye śataṁ mānuṣā ānandāḥ.

Sa eko manuṣyagandharvāṇāmānandaḥ; Śrotriyasya cākāmahatasya; Te ye śataṁ manuṣyagandharvāṇāmā-nandāḥ; Sa eko devagandharvāṇāmānandaḥ; Śrotriyasya cākāmahatasya; Te ye śataṁ devagandharvāṇāmā-nandāḥ; Sa ekaḥ pitṛṇāṁ ciralokalokānāmānandaḥ; Śrotriyasya cākāmahatasya; Te ye śataṁ pitṛṇāṁ ciralokalokānāmānandāḥ; Sa eka ājānajānāṁ devānāmā-nandaḥ.

Śrotriyasya cākāmahatasya; Te ye śatamājānajānāṁ devānāmānandāḥ; Sa ekaḥ karmadevānāṁ devānāmā-

nandaḥ; Ye karmaṇā devānapiyanti; Śrotriyasya cākāmahatasya; Te ye śataṁ karmadevānāṁ devānāmānandāḥ; Sa eko devānāmānandaḥ; Śrotriyasya cākāmahatasya; Te ye śataṁ devānāmānandāḥ; Sa eka indrasyā''nandaḥ.

Śrotriyasya cākāmahatasya; Te ye śatamindrasyā''nandāḥ; Sa eko bṛhaspaterānandaḥ; Śrotriyasya cākāmahatasya; Te ye śataṁ bṛhaspaterānandāḥ; Sa ekaḥ prajāpaterānandaḥ; Śrotriyasya cākāmahatasya; Te ye śataṁ prajāpaterānandāḥ; Sa eko brahmaṇa ānandaḥ; Śrotriyasya cākāmahatasya.

Vātaḥ, the wind; *bhīṣā,* from fear; *asmāt,* of it [i.e., of Brahman]; *pavate,* blows; *sūryaḥ,* the sun; *bhīṣā udeti,* from fear [of it] rises; *agniḥ ca,* fire also; *indraḥ ca,* as well as Indra; *mṛtyuḥ pañcamaḥ,* [and] death, the fifth; *asmāt bhīṣā,* from fear of it; *dhāvati,* each rushes [to perform its duties].

Sā eṣā ānandasya mīmāṁsā bhavati, this is what that bliss is like [of Brahman]; [just as] *yuvā syāt,* there is a young man; *sādhu-yuvā,* an honest young man; *adhyāyakaḥ,* who is well read in the scriptures; *āśiṣṭhaḥ,* has a commanding personality; *dṛḍhiṣṭhaḥ,* well built; *baliṣṭhaḥ,* very strong; *tasya iyam pṛthivī sarvā vittasya pūrṇā syāt,* if he owned the entire wealth of the whole world [i.e., if he were the emperor of the world]; *saḥ mānuṣaḥ ekaḥ ānandaḥ,* that [happiness, which is the maximum happiness anyone can conceive of for himself] is one single unit of human happiness; *te ye śatam mānuṣāḥ ānandāḥ,* that human happiness multiplied a hundred times; *saḥ,* that [happiness]; *manuṣya-gandharvāṇām ekaḥ ānandaḥ,* is the unit of happiness of the human gandharvas [men and women raised to a semi-celestial status]; *śrotriyasya ca akāmahatasya,* and of a Vedic scholar free from all desires; *te ye śatam manuṣya-gandharvāṇām ānandāḥ,* that happiness of the human gandharvas multiplied a hundred times; *saḥ deva-gandharvāṇām ekaḥ ānandaḥ,* is the unit of happiness of the deva gandharvas [persons who attain semi-celestial status by the grace of the gods and goddesses]; *śrotriyasya ca akāmahatasya,* and of a Vedic scholar free from all desires; *te ye śatam deva-gandharvāṇām ānandāḥ,* that happiness of the deva gandharvas multiplied a hundred times; *saḥ pitṛṇām ciralokalokānām ekaḥ ānandaḥ,* that is the unit of happiness of the ancestors who live in the long-lasting world reserved for them [Ciraloka, the world which lasts till the end of the current cycle of time]; *śrotriyasya ca akāmahatasya,* and of a Vedic scholar free from all desires; *te ye śatam pitṛṇām ciralokalokānām ānandāḥ,* that happiness of the ancestors living in their permanent heaven multiplied a hundred times; *saḥ ājānajānām devānām ekaḥ ānandaḥ,* that is the unit of happiness of the gods and goddesses born in the heaven called Ājāna; *śrotriyasya ca akāmahatasya,* and of a Vedic scholar free from all desires; *te ye śatam ājānajānām devānām ānandāḥ,* that happiness of the gods and goddesses born in the heaven called Ājāna multiplied a hundred times; *saḥ karmadevānām devānām ekaḥ ānandāḥ ye karmaṇā devān api yanti,* that is the unit of the happiness of the karmadevas, the gods and goddesses who attain their status through Vedic ceremonies [such as the Agnihotra sacrifice]; *śrotriyasya ca akāmahatasya,* and of a Vedic scholar free from all desires *te ye śatam karmadevānām devānām ānandāh,* that happiness of the karmadevas multiplied a hundred times; *saḥ devānām ekaḥ ānandaḥ,* that is the unit of the happiness of the gods [i.e., those gods who accept the oblations offered to a ceremonial fire]; *śrotriyasya ca akāmahatasya,* and of a Vedic scholar free from all desires; *te ye śatam devānām ānandāḥ,* that happiness of those gods multiplied a hundred times; *saḥ indrasya ekaḥ ānandaḥ,* that is the unit of the happiness of Indra [the chief of the gods and goddesses]; *śrotriyasya ca akāmahatasya,* and of a Vedic scholar free from all desires; *te ye śatam indrasya ānandāḥ,* the happiness of Indra multiplied a hundred times; *saḥ bṛhaspateḥ ekaḥ ānandaḥ,* that is the unit of happiness of Bṛhaspati [the priest of the gods and goddesses]; *śrotriyasya ca akāmahatasya,* and of a Vedic scholar free from all desires; *te ye śatam bṛhaspateḥ ānandāḥ,* the happiness of Bṛhaspati multiplied a hundred times; *saḥ prajāpateḥ ekaḥ ānandaḥ,* that is the unit of happiness of Prajāpati [i.e., Virāṭ, the sum total of all gross bodies]; *śrotriyasya ca akāmahatasya,* and of a Vedic scholar free from all desires; *te ye śatam prajāpateḥ ānandāḥ,* the happiness of Prajāpati multiplied a hundred times; *saḥ brahmaṇa ekaḥ ānandaḥ,* that is the unit of the happiness of Brahmā [i.e., Hiraṇyagarbha, the sum total of all minds]; *śrotriyasya ca akāmahatasya,* and of a Vedic scholar free from all desires.

1-4. The Wind blows out of fear of him [Brahman]. The Sun also shines out of fear. Out of fear of him Fire, Indra, and Death, the fifth, all rush to do their respective duties.

Now, to give you an idea of the happiness that Brahman represents: Take for example a young man—not merely young, but also honest, with a commanding personality, well-versed in the scriptures, well-built, and strong. Suppose he owns the wealth of the entire world. Then take this maximum happiness of his as one unit of happiness and multiply it a hundred times. That happiness then would be the unit of happiness of the human gandharvas. The happiness of the human gandharvas multiplied a hundred times would then be the unit of happiness of the deva gandharvas, and also of a Vedic scholar free from all desires. If you multiply the happiness of the deva gandharvas a hundred times, that would be the unit of happiness of the ancestors living in Ciraloka [the world which lasts till the end of the current cycle of time], and also of a Vedic scholar free from all desires. If you multiply the happiness of the ancestors living in Ciraloka a hundred times, that would be the unit of happiness of the gods and goddesses living in the Ājāna heaven, and also of a Vedic scholar free from all desires. The happiness of the gods and goddesses living in the Ājāna heaven multiplied a hundred times would then be the unit of happiness of the karmadevas [the gods and goddesses who attain divinity through the performance of the Agnihotra and other ceremonies], and also of a Vedic scholar free from all desires. If you multiply the happiness of the karmadevas a hundred times, that would be the unit of happiness of the thirty-three gods who accept oblations offered to a sacrificial fire, and also of a Vedic scholar free from all desires. The happiness of those gods multiplied a hundred times would be the unit of happiness of Indra, the chief of the gods and goddesses, and also of a Vedic scholar free from all desires. Again, if you multiply the happiness of Indra a hundred times, that would be the unit of happiness of Bṛhaspati, the priest of the gods and goddesses, and also of a Vedic scholar free from all desires. The happiness of Bṛhaspati multiplied a hundred times would be the unit of happiness of Prajāpati [i.e., Virāṭ], and also of a Vedic scholar free from all desires. Then, if you multiply the happiness of Prajāpati a hundred times, that would be the unit of happiness of Brahmā [i.e., Hiraṇyagarbha], and also of a Vedic scholar free from all desires.

At whose command does the wind blow? At the command of Brahman. Brahman is the master, the sovereign. We are often struck by the power the wind has, especially when we see the great havoc it can cause. But this wind is not free. It blows under compulsion, from fear of Brahman.

Vedānta always stresses that freedom is our goal. Human beings always feel a sense of want, of something missing. The desire for freedom is always there. Why do we build planes to fly in the air? Because we do not want to be bound to the earth. We want to be free. We are always striving to overcome the bondages and limitations of our environment.

The Upaniṣad says that even death is not free. We sometimes use the expression 'all-conquering death.' No one is free from death. It seems to be all-powerful. But death also works at the command of Brahman. The Upaniṣad is saying that everything you see in this world, even the most powerful, derives its strength from one source—Brahman.

In the Kena Upaniṣad there is a story about how once the gods became very proud. They had conquered the demons and were boasting about their great power and strength. Suddenly they saw a strange form before them. They did not know who it was, so one by one they went to investigate. First Agni, the god of fire, went. Before Agni could say anything, the apparition said, 'Who are you?' Fire answered, 'I am Agni.' 'What can you do?' 'I can burn everything in this world.' 'Then burn this piece of straw.' Agni tried and tried but could not burn it. Then Vāyu, the god of wind, went to meet the strange being. The same thing happened. When he was told to blow away the piece of straw, he could not do it. One after another all the gods went and were defeated. Then suddenly the apparition vanished, and in its place a goddess appeared. Indra, the king of the gods, asked her who the divine Being was, and she told him it was Brahman, that Brahman was the source of their power.

Śaṅkara says, '*Sarvaṁ ca jagadbhayavad dṛśyate*—the whole universe is operating on the basis of fear.'

People are always competing with each other, fighting each other, afraid of each other. One day you may be on the top of the world and the next you may be at the bottom, so you are always afraid. This is how life goes on—out of fear. And we do go on. Brahman is forcing us to function according to his will. The idea is that there is one conscious principle behind everything.

Look at the human body. There are so many organs, and each is allotted a particular role. They are all so well organized, and they work in unison. But who coordinates them? What is the coordinating factor? It is consciousness, *caitanya.* And just as there is consciousness in the human body, so also there is consciousness in this universe. Consciousness is behind everything. If this consciousness were not there, everything would collapse. And this consciousness is Brahman.

Scientists are gradually coming to realize that this universe is like a machine. You cannot destroy one part of the machine and keep the machine going. We think mosquitoes and other things are a nuisance, and we destroy them. But now they say that by destroying things we are creating a vacuum in nature. We are disturbing the balance that nature tries to maintain. We need each other. We do not realize this. We are essentially one. You cannot say that one part alone will survive and the rest should go. This universe is an integral whole, and each part has a function. Even death has a function. And who is the ruler of all this? Brahman.

Next the Upaniṣad says, let us examine the nature of bliss. We have heard that Brahman is the ruler of everything and the source of everything, but can we get any joy from Brahman? If so, what is that joy like? Now the Upaniṣad is trying to entice us to strive for Self-knowledge by giving us an idea of the bliss of Brahman. It says: 'So you think the joy from some good food is wonderful. Don't you know that the greatest of all pleasures is the joy from Self-knowledge? Let us examine this.'

What do people desire most? Ordinarily people would say, 'I want to be rich.' But being rich is not enough. If you are old then you cannot enjoy your wealth. You must be young. Then suppose you are young but you are sickly and cannot do much. So you must be young and healthy. But then you must also be intelligent and knowledgeable so that you can use your money wisely; otherwise you will squander it all.

The Upaniṣad uses the words *āśiṣṭhaḥ, dṛḍhiṣṭhaḥ,* and *baliṣṭhaḥ. Āśiṣṭhaḥ* means one who has the most commanding personality. It also means that you are quick and efficient at doing things. You are smart and disciplined. *Dṛḍhiṣṭhaḥ* means well built. *Baliṣṭhaḥ* means strong. It could also mean strong-minded. You are firm and clear in your thinking. You know what you want. You are not like a person who is always wavering and never knows what to do or what he wants.

Now, suppose you have all these qualities plus you own this entire earth with all its treasures. To most people that would be the highest form of enjoyment. But the Upaniṣad says that this is just one form of pleasure. If you multiply this form of pleasure by a hundred, you have the joy of a gandharva. A gandharva was formerly a human being but has been promoted to the status of a musician of heaven. He sings to the gods and goddesses. It is an important position, because whenever the gods assemble they must have music.

The pitṛs are our ancestors who have been very virtuous. They are said to live in Ciraloka, the world of eternity. This is relative eternity. Their life in Ciraloka lasts until the end of the cycle. Then there are different levels of gods. Some of them are minor and some major. But each level experiences a hundred times more joy than the previous one. Then you get the joy of Indra, the king of the gods. Bṛhaspati is said to be the guru of the gods and goddesses.

These gods, such as Indra, Agni, Vāyu, etc., are actually names of offices. A person who has been very good and desires such a position can be promoted to that office. Who is a god or goddess? Any good person. Whether he or she is living here in this world or in some other world, it doesn't matter.

Again and again the text says *śrotriyasya ca akāmahatasya.* A *śrotriya* is one who has studied the scriptures and knows the truth. And because he knows the truth, he is *akāmahata,* free from desires. Literally it means 'one who is not killed by desires.' *Hata* means killed. *Kāmahata* is one who is killed by desires. Desires drive us on and on so that we are no longer our own master. We become slaves to our desires. Swami Vivekananda says in one of his lectures: 'You talk about free will, but where is your free will? Can you control your mind?' If you cannot control your mind, how can you say you have free will?

But the Upaniṣad says being desireless is not enough. A table has no desires. Is that the kind of state we want? Should we live like an idiot? No, we must also be *śrotriya,* learned in the Vedas. The word *śrotriya* is derived from the word *śruti,* which refers to the Vedas. Why should we know the Vedas? Because if we have studied the scriptures, then we know what is right and what is wrong, what is good and what is not.

Now when can a person be truly *akāmahata,* free from desires? When he knows his real nature, when he knows that he is one with Brahman, which is the source of everything. Such a person does not depend on anything external for his happiness. He feels that he has everything, because he feels everything is within him. The joy of ordinary people is dependent on fulfilling certain desires or on going to a higher realm, but a person who is without desires can enjoy eternal bliss here and now, without anything external.

Śaṅkara says that even our material enjoyment—from good food, clothes, political power, etc.—comes from one source, Brahman. It is only a small part of Brahmānanda, the bliss of Brahman. He compares our material enjoyment to little drops of water that are scattered, whereas the bliss of Brahman is like the sea. All enjoyment is ānanda, bliss, but material enjoyment is impure because of the medium through which it comes. If you remove the medium, you find that the joy is all within you. You are not separate from the joy. You and joy are one. Then the drops of water become one with the sea.

Śaṅkara also says that this material enjoyment lasts only as long as the experience lasts. For instance, as long as I am eating sweets I am happy, but the moment I stop eating them my joy is gone. This kind of enjoyment is only temporary, and that is why we turn to religion. Otherwise, who would care for religion? We are all seeking permanent happiness. We go on striving for higher and higher realms, and still we are not satisfied. We are never satisfied until we know that we are one with Brahman, the source of joy.

स यश्चायं पुरुषे। यश्चासावादित्ये। स एकः। स य एवंवित्। अस्माल्लोकात्प्रेत्य। एतमन्नमयमात्मानमुपसंक्रामति। एतं प्राणमयमात्मानमुपसंक्रामति। एतं मनोमयमात्मानमुपसंक्रामति। एतं विज्ञानमयमात्मानमुपसंक्रामति। एतमानन्दमयमात्मानमुपसंक्रामति। तदप्येष श्लोको भवति॥ ५॥ इति अष्टमोऽनुवाकः॥

Sa yaścāyaṁ puruṣe; Yaścāsāvāditye; Sa ekaḥ; Sa ya evaṁvit; Asmāllokātpretya; Etamannamayamātmānamupasaṁkrāmati; Etaṁ prāṇamayamātmānamupa-

saṁkrāmati; Etaṁ manomayamātmānamupasaṁkrā mati; Etaṁ vijñānamayamātmānamupasaṁkrāmati Etamānandamayamātmānamupasaṁkrāmati; Tadapyeṣ śloko bhavati. Iti aṣṭamo'nuvākaḥ.

Saḥ yaḥ ca ayam puruṣe, he who is in this body; *yaḥ ca asau āditye,* and he who is in that sun; *saḥ ekaḥ,* he is the same; *yaḥ evamvit,* he who knows this; *saḥ,* he; *asmāt lokāt pretya,* having left this world; *etam annamayam ātmānam upasaṁkrāmati,* gets this self represented by the gross body; *etam prāṇamayam ātmānam upasaṁkrāmati,* gets this self represented by prāṇa [the vital breath]; *etam manomayam ātmānam upasaṁkrāmati,* gets this self represented by the mind; *etam vijñānamayam ātmānam upasaṁkrāmati,* gets this self represented by the intellect; *etam ānandamayam ātmānam upasaṁkrāmati,* gets this self represented by joy; *tat api eṣaḥ ślokaḥ bhavati,* here is a verse on the subject. *Iti aṣṭamaḥ anuvākaḥ,* here ends the eighth chapter.

5. He who is in this body and he who is in that sun are the same. The person who knows this and is able to turn away from this world [being free from desires], attains first the self represented by the gross body, then the self represented by the vital breath, then the self represented by the mind, then the self represented by the intellect, and then the self represented by bliss. [He then merges in the Cosmic Self, Brahman.] Here is a verse on the subject:

Sometimes Brahman is manifest, and sometimes it is not. When it manifests itself as this world, it is in every part of it. But whether manifest or not, it is present everywhere as bliss. The Upaniṣad gives the example of the sun and a human being. There is the vast, powerful sun far away. I am a small, weak human being, yet within this body is Brahman, the supreme Self. And that Self within me is also within the sun. It is the same Self—the same Self everywhere. Sri Ramakrishna used to give the analogy of pillows. Some are round and some are oblong, some are for the head and some are for the feet, but they all contain the same substance. Only the forms are different. Similarly, the same Brahman, the same Self, is everywhere only in different forms and with different names.

Śaṅkara gives the example of a pot. There is space inside the pot, and there is space outside the pot. It is the same space. Only the pot has differentiated the space. Similarly, we are like different pots. You are one, and I am another. We are conditioned by different names and forms, but in essence we are one. All living things, from Brahmā to a blade of grass, are the same Brahman. The macrocosm and the microcosm are one. This is the conclusion of the Vedānta philosophy.

Saḥ yaḥ evam vit—he who knows this. If you know this, you know Brahman. Vedānta says that the sign of ignorance is the consciousness of difference, or separation. The consciousness of oneness is knowledge. This is not just an intellectual exercise. To know is to be, according to Vedānta. If you know Brahman, you become Brahman. Sri Ramakrishna had this consciousness of oneness. He saw himself everywhere. But even just an intellectual understanding of this can help us a great deal. Our attitude towards others then changes, and we cannot hurt anyone.

Asmāt lokāt pretya—he withdraws from this phenomenal world. *Pretya* means 'withdraw.' This word is very significant. It comes from *pra* + *i*. *I* means to go, and *pra* means forward or beyond. You go beyond this world. You withdraw from this world.

How can I withdraw from the world when I have this body? Śaṅkara explains that here the Upaniṣad means you develop an attitude of non-attachment. This is what is meant by renunciation. Renunciation means not being attached to anything. You may own many things, but if you are unattached, then you have real renunciation. As Janaka, the king of Mithilā, once said, '*Mithilāyāṁ pradīptāyāṁ na me kiṁcit pradahyate*—if Mithilā burns to the ground, nothing of mine is burned.' You are indifferent, unconcerned. It is as if you are dead.

We are obsessed with the idea that this world is real. We think it is the only reality. We do not realize that it is temporary and is changing all the time. Vedānta calls it *svapnavat,* like a dream. When we dream we do not know we are dreaming. Only when we wake up do we understand that what we saw was not real. So when we understand that this world is unreal like a dream we withdraw. We say, 'Yes, this is the nature of the world.'

Now we are very much involved in this world. We identify ourselves entirely with it. But when we know what it is we see it is just fun. As Shakespeare says in his play *As You Like It:* 'All the world is a stage, and all the men and women are actors. They have their exits as well as their entrances. They come and they also go.'

Now some people object. They say, 'You are preaching escapism.' But this is not escapism. This is being pragmatic. If you know this world is ephemeral, you do not take it for granted. You may be a healthy young person today, or you may be very wealthy or have a lot of political power. But if you think things will always be like that, you are making a mistake. Some day your health will fail, and you will also get old. And at any time you may lose your wealth or power.

If you do not accept these changing conditions, you suffer. But if you are aware that changes are bound to happen, then you become detached. When you realize that the same Self is everywhere, you do not worry about anything.

What happens then? You feel your oneness with the whole universe. Even at the physical level you feel this oneness. Once when Sri Ramakrishna saw someone walking on some grass, he cried out in pain. He felt that the man was walking on his body. Another time he saw two boatmen quarrelling. When one of the boatmen started beating the other, Sri Ramakrishna felt the pain. Even the marks of the beating could be seen on his body, as if he himself had been beaten. He felt that the entire universe was his own body.

Then on the mental level you also feel this oneness. Just as we have one body, we also have one mind. The cosmic mind is sometimes compared to a lake. If there is a ripple on one part of the lake, then gradually it spreads to the rest of the lake. That is why the yogis say it is easy to know what you are thinking. Whatever you are thinking will somehow or other create a corresponding thought in others' minds.

They say that if I am at a certain level of spiritual development, I can know what is in your mind. Swamiji had this power. When Goodwin first came to record Swamiji's lectures, he did not have any regard for the philosophy. One day when he was belittling it to Swamiji, Swamiji suddenly saw the whole contents of Goodwin's mind. He saw Goodwin as a little boy and then as a young man. He saw him in different places and in different circumstances. Goodwin's life flashed before Swamiji like a movie. Then he said to Goodwin: 'Oh, I am not surprised you are talking like this. I know what you have been like in the past. Did you not do this? Were you not like this?' and so on. Goodwin fell at Swamiji's feet and surrendered himself to him.

Śaṅkara makes a lot of fuss about the word *upasaṁkrāmati.* This word literally means 'he enters into' or 'he goes into.' Śaṅkara knows that as soon as the opposition—that is, the dualists—see this word, they will say: 'That means there is somebody who goes and also some place where he goes. That means there is duality. It is like a leech, which moves from one leaf to another. It is always changing its position. If Brahman is everywhere, as the non-dualists say, how can he change his position? How can he go from one place to another?'

But Śaṅkara says there is no such thing as movement or change of position in Brahman. It is only that your ignorance is removed and you attain knowledge —knowledge that there is the same Self everywhere. Śaṅkara says in another place that it is a question of our perception. He says, if you are suffering from an eye disease, you may see two moons, but that does not make the second moon real. So also, if you have the right perception, you will not see multiplicity in this world. You will only see one. You will see the same Self everywhere.

Chapter Nine

यतो वाचो निवर्तन्ते। अप्राप्य मनसा सह। आनन्दं ब्रह्मणो विद्वान्। न बिभेति कुतश्चनेति।

एतꣳ ह वाव न तपति। किमहꣳ साधु नाकरवम्। किमहं पापमकरवमिति। स य एवं विद्वानेते आत्मानꣳ स्पृणुते। उभे ह्येवैष एते आत्मानꣳ स्पृणुते। य एवं वेद। इत्युपनिषत्॥ १॥ इति नवमोऽनुवाकः॥

Yato vāco nivartante; Aprāpya manasā saha; Ānandaṁ brahmaṇo vidvān; Na bibheti kutaścaneti.

Etaṁ ha vāva na tapati; Kimahaṁ sādhu nākaravam; Kimahaṁ pāpamakaravamiti; Sa ya evaṁ vidvānete ātmānaṁ spṛṇute; Ubhe hyevaiṣa ete ātmānaṁ spṛṇute; Ya evaṁ veda; Ityupaniṣat. Iti navamo'nuvākaḥ.

Vācaḥ, speech; *manasā saha,* with the mind; *aprāpya,* having failed to grasp; *yataḥ,* from that [Brahman]; *nivartante,* return; [anyone] *brahmaṇaḥ,* from Brahman; *ānandam vidvān,* having known bliss [as one's own Self]; *kutaścana na bibheti,* is not afraid of anyone [because there is no one besides himself].

Etam ha vāva, this kind of thought; *kim,* why; *aham sādhu na akaravam,* did I not do good things; *kim,* why; *aham pāpam akaravam,* did I do forbidden things; *iti,* this [kind of thinking in retrospect]; *na tapati,* does not prick his conscience; *saḥ,* ne; *yaḥ,* who; *ete,* these [i.e., not doing good things and doing bad things]; *evam,* as stated above; *vidvān,* having known [that they are expressions of ḥis owṇ Self]; *ātmānam spṛṇute,* comforts himself; *hi,* for; *eṣaḥ,* this [person who knows the oneness of things, knows that]; *ete,* these two [not doing good things and doing bad things]; *ubhe eva,* both; *ātmānam spṛṇute,* are one with the Self; [who is this person?]; *yaḥ evam veda,* he who knows this [oneness as the Self]; *iti upaniṣad,* this is called the Upaniṣad, the knowledge of Brahman, the secret knowledge. *Iti navamaḥ anuvākaḥ,* here ends the ninth chapter.

1. Words together with thoughts return from Brahman, unable to reach it. He who knows the bliss of Brahman is not afraid of anything or anyone [for he sees nothing but Brahman everywhere].

'Why did I not do good things?' or 'Why did I do bad things?'—such thoughts never trouble the mind of a person who has attained the knowledge of Brahman. This is because good and bad are both one to him, as they both come from Brahman, his own Self. This is the Upaniṣad, the secret knowledge.

Yataḥ vācaḥ nivartante—that from which words come back. They turn away. How can words express the Self? Can that which is finite express the infinite? No. It is beyond words, beyond thought. *Manasā saha*—the mind also cannot grasp this Brahman. You can think of something that is familiar, that is known to you, but how can you think of something about which you have had no experience at all? Our thoughts are always limited by our experience.

Ānandam brahmaṇaḥ. When you know Brahman you have bliss, because Brahman is bliss and bliss is Brahman. The Upaniṣad says the very nature of Brahman is bliss. That is why all our joy comes from Brahman, even physical joy. Brahman is the source of all joy.

Na bibheti kutaścana. A knower of the Self is not afraid of anything. When you know Brahman you have no reason to fear, because you do not see two. You see only one. You have reason to fear when there are two—you and someone else. Then you always have a doubt in your mind: The other person may be stronger than you; he may hurt you. But when you see the same Self everywhere you are not afraid.

But what about when we die? The Upaniṣad says that at the time of death an ordinary person looks back on his life and thinks of all the things he has done. He is then filled with two kinds of remorse. He thinks, 'Why did I not do good things?' Maybe he wanted to do many good things in his life, but for some reason or other he ended up never doing them. And then he thinks: 'Why did I do those bad things? I wish I had not done those things.' These kinds of thoughts nag at him.

But a person who has attained Self-knowledge has no such worry, because good and evil have ceased to exist so far as he is concerned. Śaṅkara says that for him, all differentiations are gone. These concepts of good and evil are relative, and so long as we are on the relative plane they have some meaning to us. But there comes a point when all dualities merge into one and there is nothing but Brahman.

Swami Vivekananda says that in such a state only the feeling 'I am' remains. Who am I, where am I, what am I doing?—these ideas exist only on the relative plane. When these cease, there is merely the consciousness 'I am'. Nothing else.

But what about someone who is devoted to the Personal God? Such a person has a similar experience, except that he sees his beloved Lord everywhere. No one is an enemy to him. Sri Ramakrishna used to narrate a story of a monk who was beaten unconscious by someone. When his brother monks heard about it, they went and carried him back to the monastery. After a while, the monk started to open his eyes, so his brother monks began to give him some milk. In order to see if he was fully conscious, one of the brother monks asked him, 'Who is feeding you milk?' The monk replied, 'He who beat me is now giving me milk.' To him all was God. It was the same Lord who one moment assaulted him and the next moment was nursing him.

Suppose you see nothing but Brahman everywhere. You, the one Self, are the only existence. If you are the only one existing, then good and evil cease to have any meaning. But if you accept this relative world as real, then you have to accept the concepts of good and evil.

Questions of right and wrong, good and evil, exist only in a dualistic world. A person cheats you because he thinks you are different from him. But if he knows that he is the same as you, he cannot cheat you. Can he cheat himself? That is why one who has attained the supreme knowledge of Brahman cannot do any evil. Even if he wanted to do something wrong, he couldn't.

Śaṅkara calls this knowledge *paramarahasyam,* secret. It is not meant for all because ordinary people will get confused. They will think: 'How can society go on if the distinction between good and evil is gone?' But how do we know what is good and evil? We know from the scriptures. And these scriptures are nothing but records of the lives and teachings of realized souls. Realized souls are the exemplars, the models. Because they see nothing but the one Self everywhere, whatever they do is right.

इति ब्रह्मानन्दवल्ली समाप्ता ॥

Iti brahmānandavallī samāptā.

Here ends the Brahmānanda-vallī.

PART THREE
BHṚGU-VALLĪ

Chapter One

ॐ सह नाववतु। सह नौ भुनक्तु। सह वीर्यं करवावहै। तेजस्वि नावधीतमस्तु मा विद्विषावहै॥
ॐ शान्तिः शान्तिः शान्तिः॥

Om. Saha nāvavatu; Saha nau bhunaktu; Saha vīryaṁ karavāvahai; Tejasvi nāvadhītamastu mā vidviṣāvahai. Om Śāntiḥ Śāntiḥ Śāntiḥ.

May Brahman protect us both equally. May it also give us equally the benefit of the learning. May we both work equally hard to learn. May what we learn be equally fruitful. May we never be jealous of each other. Om Peace! Peace! Peace!

भृगुर्वै वारुणिः। वरुणं पितरमुपससार। अधीहि भगवो ब्रह्मेति। तस्मा एतत्प्रोवाच। अन्नं प्राणं चक्षुः श्रोत्रं मनो वाचमिति। तꣳ होवाच। यतो वा इमानि भूतानि जायन्ते। येन जातानि जीवन्ति। यत्प्रयन्त्यभिसंविशन्ति।

तद्विजिज्ञासस्व। तद् ब्रह्मेति। स तपोऽतप्यत। स तपस्तप्त्वा॥ १॥ इति प्रथमोऽनुवाकः॥

Bhṛgurvai vāruṇiḥ; Varuṇaṁ pitaramupasasāra; Adhīhi bhagavo brahmeti; Tasmā etatprovāca; Annaṁ prāṇaṁ cakṣuḥ śrotraṁ mano vācamiti; Taṁ hovāca; Yato vā imāni bhūtāni jāyante; Yena jātāni jīvanti; Yatprayantyabhisaṁviśanti; Tadvijijñāsasva; Tad brahmeti; Sa tapo'tapyata; Sa tapastaptvā. Iti prathamo'nuvākaḥ.

Bhṛguḥ vai vāruṇiḥ, the son of Varuṇa, known as Bhṛgu; *pitaram varuṇam upasasāra,* [wanting to know about Brahman] approached his father Varuṇa [with the appropriate formalities]; *iti,* [and] said this; *bhagavaḥ,* O Lord; *brahma adhīhi,* please teach me about Brahman; *tasmai,* to him [i.e., to Bhṛgu]; *etat provāca,* [his father] said this; *annam,* food [i.e., the gross body made of food]; *prāṇam,* the life force; *cakṣuḥ,* the eyes; *śrotram,* the ears; *manaḥ,* the mind; *vācam,* the organ of speech; [he explained the functions of these organs and showed him how they help realize Brahman]; *tam ha uvāca,* he also told him [what Brahman was like]; *yataḥ,* from that [Brahman, as the source]; *vai,* by way of example; *imāni,* these; *bhūtāni,* beings [starting from Brahmā]; *jāyante,* are born; *jātāni,* having been born; *yena,* by that; *jīvanti,* are sustained; *prayanti,* proceed towards; *yat,* [into] that; *abhisaṁviśanti,* merge into; *tat,* [about] that [which is responsible for birth, sustenance, and final dissolution]; *vijijñāsasva,* ask in detail; *tat brahma iti,* please note, that is Brahman; [having heard this] *saḥ,* he

[Bhṛgu]; [in order to realize Brahman] *tapaḥ atapyata,* started practising austerities; *saḥ,* he [Bhṛgu]; *tapaḥ taptvā,* having performed austerities. *Iti prathamaḥ anuvākaḥ,* here ends the first chapter.

1. Vāruṇi, the son of Varuṇa, who was well known as Bhṛgu, once went to his father and said, 'Lord, please teach me about Brahman.' [Varuṇa felt that his son had approached him in the right manner, so] he told him about food [as the gross body], the life force, the eyes, the ears, the mind, and the organ of speech [as the knowledge of these was necessary to have some idea about Brahman]. Then, to explain the nature of Brahman, he said: 'Try to understand that Brahman is the source of everything, that everything is sustained by it, and that everything finally dissolves into it. This is Brahman.' [After hearing this,] Bhṛgu began to practise austerities. Having practised austerities, he—

The previous chapter was on the nature of Brahmānanda, the bliss of Brahman. But how do we attain Brahmānanda? This is what the present chapter is going to discuss, and it does so by introducing a story. Once a young boy named Bhṛgu came to his father, Varuṇa, and said, *'Adhīhi bhagavaḥ brahma*—O Lord, please teach me about Brahman.'

Here Bhṛgu does not address his father as 'Father.' Varuṇa is a great scholar, and as Bhṛgu is coming to him as a student, he wants to show his humility. He addresses him instead as one would address a revered teacher, as *bhagavaḥ,* Lord. It is a term of great respect. The words used in this Upaniṣad are very significant. The word *upasasāra* also indicates respect. It means to approach with humility.

Why does the Upaniṣad give a story of a father and a son? Śaṅkara says it is to show how precious this knowledge is. This knowledge is like a heritage which a father cherishes for his son. He reserves the best for his son, and the father is happy when the son asks him for it.

But Varuṇa does not immediately plunge into a discussion of Brahman without qualities and without attributes. A good teacher begins by giving simple examples, examples with which his student is familiar. All of us know the importance of food, of prāṇa, and of the eyes, ears, speech, and the mind. So Varuṇa starts by telling Bhṛgu to think of these things. Śaṅkara calls them gateways to Brahman, because if you do not have a good body, if you do not have a good mind and a sharp intellect, you cannot realize Brahman.

This body is gross. It cannot be the ultimate reality. But it is important in that it is the foundation. Without the body there can be no life, and without life there can be no mind, and without the mind there can be no intellect. And all these are our tools by which we acquire knowledge of Brahman. We cannot afford to neglect them.

But what is this Brahman? Varuṇa says that Brahman is the source of everything that exists—and Śaṅkara adds, from Brahmā to a tiny blade of grass. Then Brahman also sustains everything, and finally everything merges back into Brahman. This universe is like a vast *brahmacakra,* a wheel, or circle, of Brahman. There is birth and death. So many forms come and go, but it is all within Brahman. Everything goes back where it came from.

Śaṅkara quotes a verse from the Bṛhadāraṇyaka Upaniṣad (IV.iv.18) which says that Brahman is *prāṇasya prāṇa,* the life force of the life force. Behind this prāṇa is Brahman. Without Brahman, prāṇa cannot function. Then Brahman is *cakṣuṣaścakṣuḥ,* the eye of the eye, and *śrotrasya śrotram,* the ear of the ear. Behind the eye is the real eye; behind the ear is the real ear—and that is Brahman. Brahman makes the organs function. Śaṅkara says Brahman is *purāṇam-agryam,* the ancient one, the first cause.

Then the father says, '*Vijijñāsasva*—analyze, investigate.' The Upaniṣad does not just say *jijñāsasva,* enquire, but *vijijñāsasva,* analyze. The prefix *vi* means 'in detail.' The father says, 'Try to study this in depth.' Ultimately you have to discover the truth yourself. No one can do it for you. The father is ready to help Bhṛgu, but he knows that unless Bhṛgu exerts himself, unless he applies his own mind to the problem, it will not be clear to him. So Varuṇa says: 'I have given you an idea. Go and think about it.'

So Bhṛgu went and performed austerities. What kind of austerities? He meditated. Śaṅkara quotes a verse from the Mahābhārata which says, '*Manasaścendriyāṇāṁ ca hyaikāgryaṁ paramaṁ tapaḥ*—concentration of the mind and the sense organs is the best austerity.'

It is that by which you direct your entire mind, your sense organs, the whole of your being, to one single goal.

The mind and each of the organs has a particular power. The eye has one power, the ear another, speech another, and so on. Now these powers are scattered. They are going in all directions. Unless we can bring them to a focus—*ekāgram,* to one single point—and concentrate them, we will have no control over them.

Suppose you are trying to solve a scientific problem. In the beginning it baffles you, but you know you have to have patience. Your attitude is: 'I am not going to stop trying. I will go on trying until I succeed.' If you have a goal before you, if you have any ambition in life, then you cannot afford to be half-hearted in your attempt. You have to try heart and soul.

Śaṅkara continues: '*Tat jyāyaḥ sarvadharmebhyaḥ*—it [concentration] is superior to all other spiritual disciplines.' '*Saḥ dharmaḥ paraḥ ucyate*—it is the supreme spiritual discipline that one can undertake.' Sri Ramakrishna used to give the example of an oyster making a pearl. There is a common belief that the oyster waits for a drop of rain when the star Svāti is in the ascendant and then dives to the bottom of the ocean to form a pearl out of it. So, like that, some idea should possess us. Our thoughts, actions, everything, should be conditioned by that one idea. That is *tapasyā.* Everything else doesn't matter. It doesn't bother you. It just falls away.

This is what happened with Ramakrishna. People used to say that the Divine Mother Kālī had completely possessed him. They said that Mother Kālī was like a tigress, and Ramakrishna was her prey. He could not escape her. That is the kind of preoccupation we need for Self-realization.

So, like the oyster diving to the bottom of the ocean with its raindrop, Bhṛgu took his father's instructions and meditated on them.

Chapter Two

अन्नं ब्रह्मेति व्यजानात्। अन्नाद्ध्येव खल्विमानि भूतानि जायन्ते। अन्नेन जातानि जीवन्ति। अन्नं प्रयन्त्य-भिसंविशन्तीति। तद्विज्ञाय। पुनरेव वरुणं पितरमुपससार। अधीहि भगवो ब्रह्मेति। तꣳ होवाच। तपसा ब्रह्म विजिज्ञासस्व। तपो ब्रह्मेति। स तपोऽतप्यत। स तपस्तप्त्वा॥ १॥ इति द्वितीयोऽनुवाकः॥

Annaṁ brahmeti vyajānāt; Annāddhyeva khalvimāni bhūtāni jāyante; Annena jātāni jīvanti; Annaṁ prayantyabhisaṁviśantīti; Tadvijñāya; Punareva varuṇaṁ pitaramupasasāra; Adhīhi bhagavo brahmeti; Taṁ hovāca; Tapasā brahma vijijñāsasva; Tapo brahmeti; Sa tapo'tapyata; Sa tapastaptvā. Iti dvitīyo'nuvākaḥ.

[By performing austerities, Bhṛgu] *annam brahma iti vyajānāt,* came to know that annam, food, is Brahman; *hi,* for; *imāni bhūtāni,* all these beings [from Brahmā down to a blade of grass]; *annāt eva khalu jāyante,* are undoubtedly born from food; *jātāni,* even when born; *annena jīvanti,* they are sustained by food; [it is again food that supports them when] *prayanti,* they proceed to their end; *annam abhisaṁviśanti iti,* they finally dissolve in food also; *tat,* that [i.e., that food is Brahman]; *vijñāya,* having known [he still had some doubts]; *punaḥ eva varuṇam pitaram upasasāra,* once again he went to his father Varuṇa; *bhagavaḥ brahma adhīhi iti,* and said, O Lord, please teach me [further] about Brahman; *tam ha uvāca,* [Varuṇa] said to him; *tapasā brahma vijijñāsasva,* try to know Brahman well through austerities [i.e., by concentrating the mind on Brahman]; *tapaḥ brahma iti,* austerities and Brahman are the same; [having been instructed thus] *saḥ,* he [Bhṛgu]; *tapaḥ atapyata,* resumed his austerities; *saḥ,* he; *tapaḥ taptvā,* having practised austerities. *Iti dvitīyaḥ anuvākaḥ,* here ends the second chapter.

1. [Bhṛgu practised austerities and] came to know that food [annam] is Brahman. [Why?] Because it is from food that all beings are born. Not only that, having been born, those beings are also sustained by food. And when they perish, they dissolve into food. Bhṛgu discovered this but was not satisfied. He again approached his father [observing all the recognized formalities] and said, 'O Lord, please teach me about Brahman.' His father said: 'Practise austerities

again and try to know Brahman. Austerities and Brahman are the same.' Bhṛgu resumed his austerities, and having done so, he—

After meditating for some time, Bhṛgu came to the conclusion that *annam brahma iti,* food is Brahman. This gross world is nothing but a manifestation of Brahman. As this body has come out of food, so also this universe has come out of food. Food sustains it, and again everything merges back into food. What happens to this body when it dies? It goes back to the earth. It then becomes food for other living creatures.

So Bhṛgu went back to his father and said: 'This is what I have understood—that food is Brahman. If there is something further, please teach me that.' Śaṅkara says: 'Why did he have a doubt in his mind? Because food is seen to have birth [*annasya utpatti darśanāt*].' Can Brahman be born? If something is born, then it also dies, so it is perishable. It can't be Brahman.

But the father does not give the answer. Again he says, 'Go and meditate.' He has given the hints. A good teacher stimulates the spirit of enquiry. He makes some suggestions, but he knows that knowledge is within you. Through concentration it reveals itself.

The Upaniṣad is trying to emphasize that to attain Self-knowledge we have to work hard. We all know from experience how hard we have to work in order to pass an exam, or win a lawsuit, or get a job, or earn money. We have to pay the price for success in anything we do. How much more so if we want to attain the supreme goal of life, to realize Brahman. That is why Śaṅkara says here that we have to try again and again. Intense effort has to be made. But, as he says, we can never be satisfied until all our doubts are dispelled. And only when we realize Brahman are our doubts set at rest.

The Upaniṣad is giving an example of how a person keeps seeking. As Swami Vivekananda used to say, 'Arise, awake, and stop not till the goal is reached.' Until and unless you know your Self, until and unless you know that your Self is the Self of all that exists, that you are everywhere, that you are Brahman, you can never stop seeking.

We are constantly searching for the highest—knowingly or unknowingly. A little boy looks for the best marble on the market. A grown-up man tries to find the best automobile. And a person who is more intellectual looks for the best book or music recording on the market. We are all seeking something, but this seeking does not stop until we reach the highest, Brahman.

By introducing this story about a son going to his father to receive instructions about Brahman, the Upaniṣad is trying to draw our attention to our real identity. It says that it is a mistake if we think we are the body or the mind or the intellect. We are Spirit, the Self of the universe.

This Self is common to all of us. But this Self has different forms, some of which are gross and some of which are more subtle. We may be diverse, different from one another so far as forms are concerned, but we are all one in Spirit. To realize this oneness is our goal.

Chapter Three

प्राणो ब्रह्मेति व्यजानात्। प्राणाद्ध्येव खल्विमानि भूतानि जायन्ते। प्राणेन जातानि जीवन्ति। प्राणं प्रयन्त्यभिसंविशन्तीति। तद्विज्ञाय। पुनरेव वरुणं पितरमुपससार। अधीहि भगवो ब्रह्मेति। तꣳ होवाच। तपसा ब्रह्म विजिज्ञासस्व। तपो ब्रह्मेति। स तपोऽतप्यत। स तपस्तप्त्वा॥ १॥ इति तृतीयोऽनुवाकः॥

Prāṇo brahmeti vyajānāt; Prāṇāddhyeva khalvimāni bhūtāni jāyante; Prāṇena jātāni jīvanti; Prāṇaṁ prayantyabhisaṁviśantīti; Tadvijñāya; Punareva varuṇaṁ pitaramupasasāra; Adhīhi bhagavo brahmeti; Taṁ hovāca; Tapasā brahma vijijñāsasva; Tapo brahmeti; Sa tapo'tapyata; Sa tapastaptvā. Iti tṛtīyo'nuvākaḥ.

[As a result of his austerities, Bhṛgu] *prāṇaḥ brahma iti vyajānāt,* came to know that prāṇa [the life force] is Brahman; *hi,* for; *imāni bhūtāni khalu prāṇāt eva jāyante,* it is from prāṇa that all these beings are born; *prāṇena jātāni jīvanti,* having been born, they are sustained by prāṇa; *prāṇam prayanti abhisaṁviśanti iti,* again they go back to prāṇa and dissolve there; *tat vijñāya,* having known this; *punaḥ eva pitaram varuṇam upasasāra,* he again went back to his father Varuṇa; *bhagavaḥ adhīhi brahma iti,* O Lord, please teach me about Brahman; *tam ha uvāca,* [his father] told him; *tapasā brahma vijijñāsasva,* try to realize Brahman well through hard austerities; *tapaḥ brahma iti,* austerities and Brahman are the same; *saḥ tapaḥ atapyata,* he [Bhṛgu] resumed his austerities; *saḥ tapaḥ taptvā,* having practised austerities, he. *Iti tṛtīyaḥ anuvākaḥ,* here ends the third chapter.

1. Bhṛgu realized that prāṇa was Brahman, for it is from prāṇa that all beings have emerged. Then, having emerged, they are also sustained by it, and when they die they dissolve into it. Having known this, Bhṛgu again went to his father Varuṇa and said 'Lord, please teach me [further] about Brahman.' His father said: 'Try hard to realize Brahman through austerities. Austerities and Brahman are the same.' Bhṛgu practised austerities, and having practised them, he—

Chapter Four

मनो ब्रह्मेति व्यजानात्। मनसो ह्येव खल्विमानि भूतानि जायन्ते। मनसा जातानि जीवन्ति। मनः प्रयन्त्यभिसंविशन्तीति। तद्विज्ञाय। पुनरेव वरुणं पितर-मुपससार। अधीहि भगवो ब्रह्मेति। तꣳ होवाच। तपसा

ब्रह्म विजिज्ञासस्व। तपो ब्रह्मेति। स तपोऽतप्यत। स तपस्तप्त्वा॥१॥ इति चतुर्थोऽनुवाकः॥

Mano brahmeti vyajānāt; Manaso hyeva khalvimāni bhūtāni jāyante; Manasā jātāni jīvanti; Manaḥ prayantyabhisaṁviśantīti; Tadvijñāya; Punareva varuṇaṁ pitaramupasasāra; Adhīhi bhagavo brahmeti; Taṁ hovāca; Tapasā brahma vijijñāsasva; Tapo brahmeti; Sa tapo'tapyata; Sa tapastaptvā. Iti caturtho'nuvākaḥ.

Manaḥ brahma iti vyajānāt, [he] realized that the mind is Brahman; *manasaḥ hi eva khalu,* from the mind itself; *imāni bhūtāni jāyante,* these beings have all been born; *manasā jātāni jīvanti,* on being born, they are sustained by the mind; *manaḥ prayanti abhisaṁviśanti iti,* they return to the mind and merge with it; *tat vijñāya,* having known this; *punaḥ eva,* once again; *pitaram varuṇam upasasāra,* went back to his father Varuṇa; *bhagavaḥ adhīhi brahma iti,* [and said] Lord, please teach me about Brahman; *tam ha uvāca,* [his father] said to him; *tapasā brahma vijijñāsasva,* try your best to realize Brahman through austerities; *tapaḥ brahma iti,* the practice of austerities is Brahman; *saḥ tapaḥ atapyata,* he practised austerities [again]; *saḥ tapaḥ taptvā,* having practised austerities, he. *Iti caturthaḥ anuvākaḥ,* here ends the fourth chapter.

1. Bhṛgu realized that the mind was Brahman, as it is from the mind itself that these beings have had their birth. Having been born, they are sustained by the mind, and when they die, they go back to the mind, where they disappear. Having known this,

Bhṛgu again went back to his father Varuṇa and said, 'Lord, please teach me about Brahman.' His father replied: 'Try to understand Brahman well by practising austerities. Austerities and Brahman are the same.' Bhṛgu then practised more austerities. Having done so, he—

Slowly Bhṛgu is rising to higher levels of understanding. He started with the gross level, and then he discovered the level of the life force. Now he has come to the mental level. This is how knowledge unfolds—stage by stage.

But still Bhṛgu is not satisfied. The mind is certainly very powerful, but it also has its limitations. The mind is subject to changes and fluctuations. Sometimes it is happy, and sometimes it is unhappy. So the mind cannot be the Ultimate Reality.

Chapter Five

विज्ञानं ब्रह्मेति व्यजानात्। विज्ञानाद्ध्येव खल्विमानि भूतानि जायन्ते। विज्ञानेन जातानि जीवन्ति। विज्ञानं प्रयन्त्यभिसंविशन्तीति। तद्विज्ञाय। पुनरेव वरुणं पितर-मुपससार। अधीहि भगवो ब्रह्मेति। तꣳ होवाच। तपसा ब्रह्म विजिज्ञासस्व। तपो ब्रह्मेति। स तपोऽतप्यत। स तपस्तप्त्वा॥ १॥ इति पञ्चमोऽनुवाकः॥

Vijñānaṁ brahmeti vyajānāt; Vijñānāddhyeva khalvimāni bhūtāni jāyante; Vijñānena jātāni jīvanti; Vijñānaṁ prayantyabhisaṁviśantīti; Tadvijñāya; Punareva varuṇaṁ pitaramupasasāra; Adhīhi bhagavo brahmeti; Taṁ hovāca; Tapasā brahma vijijñāsasva; Tapo brahmeti; Sa tapo'tapyata; Sa tapastaptvā. Iti pañcamo-'nuvākaḥ.

Vijñānam brahma iti vyajānāt, [Bhṛgu] realized that the intellect is Brahman; *vijñānāt hi eva khalu,* it is from the mind itself; *imāni bhūtāni jāyante,* these beings are born; *vijñānena jātāni jīvanti,* having been born, they are sustained by the intellect; *vijñānam prayanti abhisaṁviśanti iti,* they return to the intellect and merge into it; *tat vijñāya,* having known this; *punaḥ eva,* again; *pitaram varuṇam upasasāra,* [Bhṛgu] went back to his father Varuṇa; *bhagavaḥ adhīhi brahma iti,* [and said] O Lord, please teach me about Brahman; *tam ha uvāca,* [his father] told him; *tapasā brahma vijijñāsasva,* try to know Brahman well through austerities; *tapaḥ brahma iti,* the practice of austerities is Brahman; *saḥ tapaḥ atapyata,* he [again] practised austerities; *saḥ tapaḥ taptvā,* having practised austerities, he. *Iti pañcamaḥ anuvākaḥ,* here ends the fifth chapter.

1. Bhṛgu then came to know that the intellect is Brahman. All beings that exist are born from the intellect. Having been born, they are looked after by the intellect. And as they die, they go back to the intellect and merge in it. Having known this, Bhṛgu again went back to his father Varuṇa and said, 'Lord, please teach me about Brahman.' Varuṇa

replied: 'Try to know Brahman well through austerities. The practice of austerities is nothing but Brahman.' Bhṛgu practised austerities, and having done so, he—

The intellect is also a kind of reality. The intellect determines what is right and wrong, and what is good and bad, but it also changes. Today we may think one thing is right and tomorrow we may think something else. As we get more experience our concepts change. We become wiser and more mature. But our intellectual level does not necessarily grow with age. We find that some people may be old in years, but they are still not mature, and other people may not be very old, but they are thoughtful and mature. So the intellect also cannot be the final reality because of its changing nature.

Chapter Six

आनन्दो ब्रह्मेति व्यजानात्। आनन्दाद्ध्येव खल्विमानि भूतानि जायन्ते। आनन्देन जातानि जीवन्ति। आनन्दं प्रयन्त्यभिसंविशन्तीति। सैषा भार्गवी वारुणी विद्या। परमे व्योमन्प्रतिष्ठिता। स य एवं वेद प्रतितिष्ठति। अन्नवानन्नादो भवति। महान्भवति प्रजया पशुभिर्ब्रह्म-वर्चसेन। महान् कीर्त्या॥ १॥ इति षष्ठोऽनुवाकः॥

Ānando brahmeti vyajānāt; Ānandāddhyeva khalvimāni bhūtāni jāyante; Ānandena jātāni jīvanti; Ānandaṁ prayantyabhisaṁviśantīti; Saiṣā bhārgavī vāruṇī vidyā; Parame vyomanpratiṣṭhitā; Sa ya evaṁ veda pratitiṣṭhati; Annavānannādo bhavati; Mahānbhavati prajayā paśubhirbrahmavarcasena; Mahān kīrtyā. Iti ṣaṣṭho'nuvākaḥ.

Ānandaḥ brahma iti vyajānāt, [Bhṛgu] came to know that bliss is Brahman; *ānandāt hi eva khalu,* it is from bliss; *imāni bhūtāni jāyante,* these beings are born; *ānandena jātāni jīvanti,* having been born, they are sustained by bliss; *ānandam prayanti abhisaṁviśanti iti,* they return to bliss and also merge into it; *sā eṣā,* here is; *bhārgavī vāruṇī vidyā,* the knowledge which Bhṛgu attained, acquired from Varuṇa; *parame vyoman pratiṣṭhitā,* resting in the empty space of the heart; *yaḥ evam veda,* he who knows [Brahman] as such; *saḥ pratitiṣṭhati,* is rooted [in Brahman]; *annavān annādaḥ bhavati,* he has much food at his disposal and also enjoys much food [i.e., having been united with Brahman he has everything at his command—from gross food to the finest bliss]; *mahān bhavati,* he becomes great; *prajayā,* by many children; *paśubhiḥ,* by many animals; *brahmavarcasena,* by the glow of the light of Brahman; *kīrtyā mahān,* he has much fame. *Iti ṣaṣṭhaḥ anuvākaḥ,* here ends the sixth chapter.

1. Bhṛgu came to know that bliss is Brahman, for it is from bliss that all these beings are born. Having been born, they are supported by bliss, and when they perish, they go back to bliss and disappear

into it. Bhṛgu learned this from Varuṇa, who taught him this Truth. This Truth is in the empty space of the heart. [It encompasses everything from gross food up to subtle bliss]. He who knows this is established in the bliss of Brahman. He also possesses much food and is capable of eating much food [i.e., he is like fire, consuming everything]. He has many children and posseses many animals, and he radiates the power of Brahman. He is indeed great. His fame spreads far.

So gradually, through stages, Bhṛgu arrives at the Ultimate Reality. The idea is that the Upaniṣad does not want you to accept anything unless you find it rational and logical. You must question and think and meditate. Śaṅkara says, '*Śanaiḥ śanaiḥ antaḥ anupraviśya*—step by step you enter within.' You penetrate (*anupraviśya*), or probe, into the depths of your consciousness.

Why does the Upaniṣad use the word *tapasyā,* austerity? Why does it not just say 'think' or 'meditate'? Because it wants to emphasize that this is disciplined thinking. All of us think. We cannot help but think. But most of us think very superficially. We think illogically, not step by step. We cannot control the mind, so we cannot concentrate on anything. This is why Śaṅkara says *śanaiḥ śanaiḥ,* step by step. It must be disciplined thinking.

Suppose you are a scientist engaged in some kind of research. Every bit of data at every step you must note down and take into account. You cannot afford to ignore anything. This is also a kind of *tapasyā.*

Through *tapasyā,* Bhṛgu came to realize that bliss, *ānanda,* is Brahman. And that bliss is *parame vyoman,* within the supreme space in the heart. Śaṅkara says it is *antaratama,* the innermost. It is hidden deep within yourself.

What happens to a person who realizes this bliss? The Upaniṣad says that he becomes an eater of food. That is to say, he enjoys not only spiritual bliss, but also this physical universe. He enjoys everything. Spiritual knowledge gives a person self-confidence, strength of mind, and strength of will, and with these qualities a person can attain anything.

Then also, *mahān bhavati*—he becomes great. In what sense? The Upaniṣad says here, in every sense—even in terms of his children and animals. In those days animals represented wealth, so the Upaniṣad means that in respect of wealth he becomes great. Then also, his children become great because they have a share in their father's knowledge.

But all this is insignificant compared with *brahmavarcasa,* the light, or glow, of Brahman. *Brahmavarcasa* is a spiritual radiance that comes from the bliss within. It does not come from anything external. Once a man from Europe was looking at a picture of Swami Vivekananda. He said: 'Why does he look so happy? There is so much sorrow and suffering in this world, and he looks so complacent.' Some people think that saints should look very depressed and pensive. It is true that there is sorrow in this world. And it is not that these saints think this sorrow should continue. But there is joy also, and that joy is the Ultimate Reality which is within us, which becomes manifest when we attain Self-knowledge. In the last part of his life Sri Ramakrishna suffered greatly from cancer, yet his face glowed with divine joy. Nothing could take that joy away.

Then also, a person who has realized Brahman becomes great in spiritual qualities. What are these spiritual qualities? Śaṅkara says they are *śama-dama-jñānādi,* self-control, self-restraint, knowledge, or wisdom, and so forth. How do we judge a person's spiritual attainments? What is the criterion of spirituality? Sometimes we hear about a person having miraculous powers. Is that spirituality? Śaṅkara says no. Spirituality is to be judged in terms of character. He says a person becomes great through his moral conduct (*śubhapracāranimittayā*). He always does good to others. In the final analysis, this is the test of spirituality. There is no other test.

Chapter Seven

अन्नं न निन्द्यात्। तद्व्रतम्। प्राणो वा अन्नम्। शरीरमन्नादम्। प्राणे शरीरं प्रतिष्ठितम्। शरीरे प्राणः प्रतिष्ठितः। तदेतदन्नमन्ने प्रतिष्ठितम्। स य एतदन्नमन्ने प्रतिष्ठितं वेद प्रतितिष्ठति। अन्नवानन्नादो भवति।

महान्भवति प्रजया पशुभिर्ब्रह्मवर्चसेन। महान् कीर्त्या॥ १॥
इति सप्तमोऽनुवाकः॥

Annaṁ na nindyāt; Tadvratam; Prāṇo vā annam; Śarīramannādam; Prāṇe śarīraṁ pratiṣṭhitam; Śarīre prāṇaḥ pratiṣṭhitaḥ; Tadetadannamanne pratiṣṭhitam; Sa ya etadannamanne pratiṣṭhitaṁ veda pratitiṣṭhati; Annavānannādo bhavati; Mahānbhavati prajayā paśubhirbrahmavarcasena; Mahān kīrtyā. Iti saptamo'nuvākaḥ.

Annam na nindyāt, he will never find fault with anna [food]; *tat vratam,* [to one who knows Brahman] it is like a holy rule; *prāṇaḥ vai annam,* life is food [for food supports life]; *śarīram annādam,* the body consumes the food; *prāṇe śarīram pratiṣṭhitam,* the body is supported by prāṇa, the life force; *śarīre prāṇaḥ pratiṣṭhitaḥ,* prāṇa is supported by the body; *tat etat,* it is like this [both the body and life]; *annam anne pratiṣṭhitam,* the body is dependent on life; *saḥ yaḥ,* anyone who; *etat veda,* knows this; *annam anne pratiṣṭhitam,* that the body is dependent on life; *pratitiṣṭhati,* becomes world famous; *annavān annādaḥ bhavati,* he possesses much food and also greatly enjoys food; *prajayā paśubhiḥ brahmavarcasena mahān bhavati,* he becomes famous for his children, for the great amount of animal wealth he owns, and for his radiance arising from the knowledge of Brahman; *kīrtyā mahān,* he is acknowledged as one of the greatest teachers of spiritual truths. *Iti saptamaḥ anuvākaḥ,* here ends the seventh chapter.

1. [He who knows Brahman and understands the important role that food plays] will never speak ill of food. This is like a religious vow with him. Life is food. The body consumes that food [so it is called *annāda,* the eater]. The body is alive because of life, and is therefore dependent on life. But life is also dependent on the body. Both are dependent on each other [as if one kind of anna, or food, is dependent on another]. One who knows both these 'annas' [the body and life] as dependent on each other, becomes world famous. He possesses large quantities of food, and he also greatly enjoys eating. He has many children and a vast amount of animal wealth, and he also shines with the glow of spiritual knowledge. He is highly respected thereby and is well known as a teacher of spiritual truths.

Now anna is being praised. Anna has two meanings here. Literally it means food. But it also means this gross, physical universe. Why? Because this universe is the product of food. So the Upaniṣad says you must not neglect anna. Many people think that Vedānta is other-worldly, that it wants you to think of the other world and not of this one. But here you find that the Upaniṣad is saying that this world is important. You need this physical world. You need this human body. You need food. In fact, it is our religious duty (*vrata*) to take care of them and not neglect them.

Prāṇaḥ vai annam—this prāṇa is also anna. The body and the life force are interconnected, interdependent. Life cannot exist without the body, and the body cannot exist without life. What is the body without life? It is just a mass of flesh that will decompose.

Śarīram annādam. This body can survive only through food so the body is called *annādam,* the eater. Both life and the body are dependent on food, and therefore food should not be belittled or neglected. Only that person survives who knows the importance of food.

Why is so much importance given to food? Śaṅkara says it is because food is the gateway to the knowledge of Brahman. Without food you cannot have a healthy body, and if you want to make any progress in life, you must have a healthy body. It is the first step.

Chapter Eight

अन्नं न परिचक्षीत। तद्व्रतम्। आपो वा अन्नम्। ज्योतिरन्नादम्। अप्सु ज्योतिः प्रतिष्ठितम्। ज्योतिष्यापः प्रतिष्ठिताः। तदेतदन्नमन्ने प्रतिष्ठितम्। स य एतदन्नमन्ने प्रतिष्ठितं वेद प्रतितिष्ठति। अन्नवानन्नादो भवति। महान्भवति प्रजया पशुभिर्ब्रह्मवर्चसेन। महान्कीर्त्या॥ १॥

इति अष्टमोऽनुवाकः॥

Annaṁ na paricakṣīta; Tadvratam; Āpo vā aṇnam; Jyotirannādam; Apsu jyotiḥ pratiṣṭhitam; Jyotiṣyāpaḥ pratiṣṭhitāḥ; Tadetadannamanne pratiṣṭhitam; Sa ya etadannamanne pratiṣṭhitaṁ veda pratitiṣṭhati; Annavānannādo bhavati; Mahānbhavati prajayā paśubhirbrahmavarcasena; Mahānkīrtyā. Iti aṣṭamo'nuvākaḥ.

Annam na paricakṣīta, one should not neglect anna [food]; *tat vratam,* this is like a religious injunction; [But what is anna?]; *āpaḥ vai annam,* water itself is anna; *jyotiḥ annādam,* energy [or, fire, etc.] is that which consumes food; *apsu jyotiḥ pratiṣṭhitam,* [at the same time] energy is inherent in water; *āpaḥ jyotiṣi pratiṣṭhitāḥ,* water is also inherent in energy, fire, etc.; *tat etat annam anne pratiṣṭhitam,* both these variants of anna are dependent on each other; *saḥ yaḥ etat annam anne pratiṣṭhitam veda,* he who knows the secret of one form of anna depending on another; *pratitiṣṭhati,* becomes successful; *annavān annādaḥ bhavati,* he possesses much food and also greatly enjoys food; *prajayā paśubhiḥ brahmavarcasena mahān bhavati,* he becomes famous for his children, for the great amount of animal wealth he owns, and for his radiance arising from the knowledge of Brahman; *kīrtyā mahān,* he distinguishes himself as a spiritual teacher. *Iti aṣṭamaḥ anuvākaḥ,* here ends the eighth chapter.

1. One should not neglect food. Consider this as a religious injunction. [But what is 'food'?] Water is nothing but food, and fire consumes that food [so it is called *annādam*]. There is fire [or, energy] in water. There is also water in fire. This is an example of food being dependent on food. One who knows this principle of one kind of food being

dependent on another, becomes highly successful. He possesses large quantities of food, and he also greatly enjoys eating. He has many children and a vast amount of animal wealth, and he also shines with the glow of spiritual knowledge. He is highly respected thereby and is well known as a spiritual teacher.

This physical universe, according to Hindu philosophy, is constituted of five elements: space, air, fire, water, and earth. These elements are interrelated, interconnected. They support one another. And they are all important to us. If you want to make any progress in your spiritual life, the entire environment must be congenial. You must have pure air, pure water, pure food, and you must have fire. If it is too cold, or if there is too much noise, or if the wind is blowing too much, it is difficult to meditate. We often find that if we go to a beautiful, quiet place in the mountains or near a river, we immediately feel like sitting down and meditating. At once the mind becomes quiet and indrawn.

Apsu jyotiḥ pratiṣṭhitam. It may seem strange that fire and water are related, that fire would be said to be in water. This idea may come from the common experience of seeing lightning in rain clouds. But the word *jyoti* could also mean energy. There is energy in water. Electricity is often produced from running water.

The point that this portion of the Upaniṣad is trying to make is that you cannot afford to neglect this physical universe. It is good if you are seeking spiritual bliss. That is the goal. But to get this bliss you have to have a healthy body and a healthy environment. You have to look after this universe. When the Upaniṣads say that the world is unreal, it does not mean that you can ignore it and dismiss it altogether. This world is very much necessary. But then you must see it as a manifestation of Brahman.

What the Upaniṣad is saying is to think of these things—food, the mind, the physical universe with the various elements, etc.—as Brahman. Know them as Brahman, and respect them, take care of them. They are nothing but Brahman. Brahman by its nature is ānanda, bliss, but you have to take care of these other things as well because they are the basis, the foundation, on which you struggle and eventually realize Brahman.

As Swami Vivekananda says, the means are as important as the end. Take care of the means. Put the chemicals together. Then you will have the desired result. All these factors—the environment, the body, the mind, the intellect—are vital. If they are properly taken care of, you will then attain the goal, which is Brahman.

Chapter Nine

अन्नं बहु कुर्वीत। तद्व्रतम्। पृथिवी वा अन्नम्। आकाशोऽन्नादः। पृथिव्यामाकाशः प्रतिष्ठितः। आकाशे पृथिवी प्रतिष्ठिता। तदेतदन्नमन्ने प्रतिष्ठितम्। स य एतदन्नमन्ने

प्रतिष्ठितं वेद प्रतितिष्ठति। अन्नवानन्नादो भवति। महान्भवति प्रजया पशुभिर्ब्रह्मवर्चसेन। महान् कीर्त्या॥ १ ॥
इति नवमोऽनुवाकः॥

Annaṁ bahu kurvīta; Tadvratam; Pṛthivī vā annam; Ākāśo'nnādaḥ; Pṛthivyāmākāśaḥ pratiṣṭhitaḥ; Ākāśe pṛthivī pratiṣṭhitā; Tadetadannamanne pratiṣṭhitam; Sa ya etadannamanne pratiṣṭhitaṁ veda pratitiṣṭhati; Annavānannādo bhavati; Mahānbhavati prajayā paśubhirbrahmavarcasena; Mahān kīrtyā. Iti navamo'nuvākaḥ.

Annam bahu kurvīta, try to multiply anna [food]; *tat,* doing so; *vratam,* is a religious duty [for all]; [But what is anna?]; *pṛthivī vai annam,* this earth is food; *ākāśaḥ annādaḥ,* the sky swallows [envelops] the earth; *ākāśaḥ pṛthivyām pratiṣṭhitaḥ,* the sky is in the earth [being all-pervasive]; *pṛthivī ākāśe pratiṣṭhitā,* the earth is [also] in the sky; *tat etat,* in this way; *annam anne pratiṣṭhitam,* one kind of anna is dependent on another; *saḥ yaḥ etat annam anne pratiṣṭhitam veda,* he who knows [the secret of] one form of anna depending on another; *pratitiṣṭhati,* succeeds in life; *annavān annādaḥ bhavati,* he possesses much food and also greatly enjoys food; *prajayā paśubhiḥ brahmavarcasena mahān bhavati,* he becomes famous for his children, for the great amount of animal wealth he owns, and for his radiance arising from the knowledge of Brahman; *kīrtyā mahān,* he distinguishes himself as a spiritual teacher. *Iti navamaḥ anuvākaḥ,* here ends the ninth chapter.

1. One should try to increase the quantity of food one has. This is a religious duty. [But what is 'food'?] The earth is the food. The sky eats this food [so it is called *annāda,* the eater]. The sky is dependent on the earth. The earth is also dependent on the sky. They are both interdependent, one kind of food depending on another. One who knows this principle of one kind of food being dependent on another, becomes highly successful. He possesses large quantities of food, and he also greatly enjoys eating. He has many children and a vast amount of animal wealth, and he also shines with the glow of spiritual knowledge. He is highly respected thereby and is well esteemed as a spiritual teacher.

Chapter Ten

न कंचन वसतौ प्रत्याचक्षीत। तद्व्रतम्। तस्माद्यया कया च विधया बह्वन्नं प्राप्नुयात्। अराध्यस्मा अन्नमित्याचक्षते। एतद्वै मुखतोऽन्नꣳ राद्धम्। मुखतोऽस्मा अन्नꣳ राध्यते। एतद्वै मध्यतोऽन्नꣳ राद्धम्। मध्यतोऽस्मा अन्नꣳ राध्यते। एतद्वा अन्ततोऽन्नꣳ राद्धम्। अन्ततोऽस्मा अन्नꣳ राध्यते॥ १॥

Na kaṁcana vasatau pratyācakṣīta; Tadvratam; Tasmādyayā kayā ca vidhayā bahvannaṁ prāpnuyāt; Arādhyasmā annamityācakṣate; Etadvai mukhato'nnaṁ rāddham; Mukhato'smā annaṁ rādhyate; Etadvai madhyato'nnaṁ rāddham; Madhyato'smā annaṁ rādhyate; Etadvā antato'nnaṁ rāddham; Antato'smā annaṁ rādhyate.

Vasatau kaṁcana, if anyone asks for shelter [in your house]; *na pratyācakṣīta,* don't turn him away; *tat vratam,* this is a religious obligation; *tasmāt yayā kayā ca vidhayā,* therefore by any means; *bahu annam prāpnuyāt,* one should keep plenty of food [ready so that there is no difficulty in feeding guests when they come]; [a far-sighted person who has saved food for guests] *asmai annam arādhi iti ācakṣate,* will say to them, I have saved food [in anticipation of your coming]; *etat vai annam,* this food [I am giving you]; *mukhataḥ rāddham,* was procured by the excellence of my own skill [or, in my early years]; [as a result of this] *asmai,* to him [i.e., to the host]; *annam mukhataḥ rādhyate,* food will return to him by virtue of the same excellence of skill [or, in his early years]; *etat vai annam madhyataḥ rāddham,* [but suppose] this food was acquired by means that were not so good; *asmai annam madhyataḥ rādhyate,* the food will return to him in the same manner; *etat vai annam antataḥ rāddham,* [but suppose] this food was acquired by bad means; *asmai annam antataḥ rādhyate,* the food will return to him in the same manner.

1. If someone comes and asks for a place to stay, one should not turn him away. This is a religious obligation. [And if there is a guest, it is necessary to provide him his needs.] This is why wise people

say that one should procure food by whatever means necessary. It is as if it has been acquired in anticipation of the guest. This is what wise people say. As the person gives the food he makes it clear that he procured the food by excellent means—i.e., by the skill of his profession. He is then duly rewarded for this gift in that the food returns to him through excellent means. If he procured the food by means that were not so good—i.e., not entirely by his own skill, but by a mixture of skill and bad means—then the food returns to him in the same manner. If, however, he has adopted bad means to procure the food for his guest, the food will return to him in the same manner.

The Upaniṣad has just said that the sky and the earth are made of the same matter and that they are interdependent. So, knowing this—that everything is interdependent—means that you have an obligation to fulfil: you can never turn away guests who seek shelter at your place. And if you accept them as guests, you must also provide them with food. The Upaniṣad says you should greet them as if you were expecting them and say to them that you have been saving food for them. It is necessary then for you to save plenty of food, so that when guests come you have no difficulty in feeding them.

Feeding others has its own reward, because food returns to you about the same time and in the same manner as you gave it. In fact, no gift you make goes unrewarded. The features your gift has mark the reward you receive.

य एवं वेद। क्षेम इति वाचि। योगक्षेम इति प्राणापानयोः। कर्मेति हस्तयोः। गतिरिति पादयोः। विमुक्तिरिति पायौ। इति मानुषीः समाज्ञाः। अथ दैवीः। तृप्तिरिति वृष्टौ। बलमिति विद्युति॥ २॥

Ya evaṁ veda; Kṣema iti vāci; Yogakṣema iti prāṇāpānayoḥ; Karmeti hastayoḥ; Gatiriti pādayoḥ; Vimuktiriti pāyau; Iti mānuṣīḥ samājñāḥ; Atha daivīḥ; Tṛptiriti vṛṣṭau; Balamiti vidyuti.

Yaḥ evam veda, he who knows thus [i.e., the importance of food and the merits of giving it to others, gets rewarded as stated earlier]; [Now, a discussion on Brahman and its relationship with other things:] *kṣemaḥ,* self-restraint [lit., saving what you have already acquired]; *vāci iti,* as evident in speech [i.e., try to feel Brahman present in things you save]; *prāṇāpānayoḥ yogakṣemaḥ iti,* [as present] in what you add and what you save in breathing; *hastayoḥ karma iti,* [as present] in hands as whatever you do; *pādayoḥ gatiḥ iti,* [as present] in legs as movement; *pāyau vimuktiḥ iti,* [as present even] in discharges from the anus; *iti mānuṣīḥ samājñāḥ,* thus in all human activities; *atha daivīḥ,* next, in all divine [i.e., natural] phenomena; *vṛṣṭau tṛptiḥ iti,* as the relief you feel from rain [for giving good crops and other things]; *vidyuti balam iti,* as power in lightning.

2. He who knows thus [i.e., the importance of food and the merits of giving it, gets the results as described].

[One should try to see Brahman] as restraint in speech; as what you add and what you save in the expansion and contraction of your breath; in the work you do with your hands; in the movements you make with your feet; and in the discharge from your anus. [Brahman is in all these, and] these activities are all ways of worship at the human level. Now, about worship at the divine level [or, at the level of natural forces]: Imagine Brahman in the relief you get from rain [which brings good crops and other things] and in the power in lightning.

The Upaniṣad is now discussing practical religion. Earlier the philosophy was discussed, but how do we apply that philosophy? We must treat everything as Brahman.

Then the Upaniṣad says that even our physical functions—our speech, our breathing and other functions of the organs—should be regarded as sacred. Just as we consider our wealth or property as valuable and we try to preserve it, so also we should consider our speech and other functions as valuable. They should be preserved and not wasted. And when we preserve something, that means we also try to increase it and add to it. When we increase our breathing, we also increase our span of life and our physical strength. In those days, much importance was attached to breathing. Good breathing gives you stamina and keeps your body and organs in good health. It is an aid to Self-realization.

The Muṇḍaka Upaniṣad says, *'Nāyamātmā balahīnena*

labhyaḥ—this Self cannot be known by the weak.' A person who is physically weak cannot make any progress. He cannot even earn his own livelihood. And spiritual struggle is much more difficult than earning your livelihood. How can you do it if you do not have a good body?

The Upaniṣad is reminding us that all the functions of the body are important. We need good hands and legs in order to work. Then, even our organs of elimination are important, because if they do not work properly we cannot stay in good health.

Mānuṣīḥ means with reference to the human being, the human body. *Samājñāḥ* literally means perceptions, but here the word is used in the sense of *upāsanā,* worship, or meditation. We must remember that all our organs—our speech, hands, feet, everything—should be directed to the attainment of Self-knowledge. If that is our goal, our motive, then everything becomes worship.

Then *daivīḥ* means with reference to nature. Rain and lightning are phenomena of nature. Can nature exist without Brahman? It is also Brahman. The Upaniṣad is saying that everything that happens, either with reference to the human being or with reference to nature, is related to Brahman. Everything is spiritual.

यश इति पशुषु। ज्योतिरिति नक्षत्रेषु। प्रजाति-
रमृतमानन्द इत्युपस्थे। सर्वमित्याकाशे। तत्प्रतिष्ठेत्युपासीत।

प्रतिष्ठावान् भवति। तन्मह इत्युपासीत। महान्भवति। तन्मन इत्युपासीत। मानवान्भवति॥ ३॥

Yaśa iti paśuṣu; Jyotiriti nakṣatreṣu; Prajātiramṛtamānanda ityupasthe; Sarvamityākāśe; Tatpratiṣthetyupāsīta; Pratiṣṭhāvān bhavati; Tanmaha ityupāsīta; Mahānbhavati; Tanmana ityupāsīta; Mānavānbhavati.

Yaśaḥ iti paśuṣu, fame based on the number of animals possessed [because animals represent wealth]; *jyotiḥ iti nakṣatreṣu,* light in the stars; *upasthe,* in the organ of procreation; *prajātiḥ amṛtam ānandaḥ iti,* having children as a way of immortality and the joy of it [i.e., Brahman is everywhere and in everything—think of this and you will be happy]; *ākāśe sarvam iti,* everything rests in space [i.e., all that exists in space is Brahman]; *tat,* that [Brahman]; *pratiṣṭhā,* the support of everything; *iti upāsīta,* worship it as such; [the result of such worship is that] *pratiṣṭhāvān bhavati,* the person [who worships thus] himself becomes the support of everything; *tat,* that [Brahman]; *mahaḥ iti,* as the greatest; *upāsīta,* worship; [in doing so] *mahān bhavati,* he [the worshipper] himself becomes great; *tat,* that [Brahman]; *manaḥ iti upāsīta,* fills the mind and worship it as such; [in doing so] *mānavān bhavati,* he [the worshipper] becomes a thoughtful [or, discerning] person.

3. [Brahman is in everything—] in the fame a person has because of the number of animals he owns, in the light of the stars, in the organ of procreation, and in the joy of the prospect of attaining immortality

through children. One should worship Brahman as the support of everything in space. If a person worships Brahman as such, he himself becomes the support of everything. One should worship Brahman as the greatest. If a person does so, he himself becomes the greatest. One should worship Brahman as the mind. A person who does so will have a very thoughtful mind.

In those days, animals, especially cattle, represented wealth. Even in recent times a person was considered rich if he had many cows, horses, and maybe some elephants. A person's fame, then, would rest on how many animals he had.

Having children also was considered to be good fortune, because in a sense it makes you immortal. You continue to live in them. This is why people get such joy in having children.

The entire universe rests on Brahman, so the Upaniṣad says to think of Brahman as the support, the foundation, of everything. If you think of Brahman in this way, you become that support—you become Brahman.

Similarly, if you worship Brahman as *maha,* great, you become great. You may or may not accept this, but it is a wonderful idea. Śaṅkara quotes a verse from the Mudgala Upaniṣad (III.3): '*Tam yathā yathā upāsate tadeva bhavati*—as a person worships him, so he becomes.' If you think of God as somebody very kind, you become kind.

Why do we worship a particular form of God? Because

we are trying to be like that form of God. They say, the more you think of a particular deity the nearer you get to him—not only spiritually, even physically. For instance, Śiva is a symbol of certain characteristics. He is very generous, very kind, always forgiving, very simple and selfless. You may offend him, but he immediately forgets it. Now suppose you worship Śiva and think of him all the time. Eventually you become like him. You acquire the same characteristics.

Then suppose you worship Brahman as the mind, or as the power of the intellect. You will then also become intellectually great. Your mental powers will grow.

You see, now you are an individual. You have your body, your mind, your intellect, and these are limitations. They have separated you from the cosmos. But if you can transcend your body, mind, and intellect, you are then in touch with the cosmos. The Upaniṣad is saying that just as we are first physical, then mental, and then intellectual, so also, Brahman is physical, mental, and so on.

For example, the human body is made up of millions of cells. These cells each have an independent existence, yet they are all part of the human body. If you die, the cells that constitute your body will also die. They cannot live without you. Similarly, all the human beings, plants, and animals are like so many cells, as it were, of the cosmic body of Brahman. But this is just the physical aspect. There is the mental aspect also, the cosmic mind. You have your mind;

I have my mind. But there is a cosmic mind, and our minds are fragments of that cosmic mind.

We do not realize that we have such a large dimension to ourselves. We are only conscious of our small mind. But once in a while we discover within ourselves layers of consciousness that we did not know were there. We find that we can grasp thoughts which are much finer and subtler than we thought we could. Now our minds are controlled by our ego consciousness. But if we can overcome that ego consciousness, if we can wipe out that little self and project ourselves to a higher level, then we can become one with the cosmos.

तन्नम इत्युपासीत। नम्यन्तेऽस्मै कामाः। तद्ब्रह्मे-
त्युपासीत। ब्रह्मवान्भवति। तद्ब्रह्मणः परिमर इत्युपासीत।
पर्येणं म्रियन्ते द्विषन्तः सपत्नाः। परि येऽप्रिया भ्रातृव्याः।
स यश्चायं पुरुषे। यश्चासावादित्ये। स एकः॥ ४॥

Tannama ityupāsīta; Namyante'smai kāmāḥ; Tadbrahmetyupāsīta; Brahmavānbhavati; Tadbrahmaṇaḥ parimara ityupāsīta; Paryeṇaṁ mriyante dviṣantaḥ sapatnāḥ; Pari ye'priyā bhrātṛvyāḥ; Sa yaścāyaṁ puruṣe; Yaścāsāvāditye; Sa ekaḥ.

Tat namaḥ iti upāsīta, one should worship him with the respect due to him; *asmai kāmāḥ namyante,* to him [who so worships] all that he desires comes to him of themselves; *tat brahma iti upāsīta,* one should worship him as Brahman; [if one does so] *brahmavān bhavati,* he becomes Brahman himself; *tat,* him; *brahmaṇaḥ parimaraḥ iti upāsīta,* one should worship as Brahman's place to kill [i.e., space]; *enam dviṣantaḥ sapatnāḥ,* those rivals who are jealous of him; *pari mriyante,* perish; *ye apriyāḥ bhrātṛvyāḥ pari* [*mriyante*], [and] those who are hostile to him also perish; *saḥ yaḥ ca ayam puruṣe,* he who is in this body; *yaḥ ca asau āditye,* he who is in that sun; *saḥ ekaḥ,* he is the same.

4. One should worship him as deserving the highest adoration. If a person does so, whatever desires he has will come to him. One should regard him as supreme. If a person does so, he himself will become supreme [i.e., he will become Brahman, 'the greatest']. One should regard him as space, where all natural forces [rain, lightning, etc.] merge into Brahman. This way he will get rid of all those who are jealous of or otherwise ill-disposed towards him. He who is within this body and he who is within that solar orb above are one and the same.

The Upaniṣad says if you worship Brahman as *nama,* adoration, all your desires will adore you. They will come and surrender to you. They will pay their respects to you and say, 'We are at your service.' This is a paradox. If you say, 'I want money,' you won't get money. But when you have the feeling, 'I want Brahman, only Brahman,' you find everything comes to you. Why? Because Brahman is the source of everything.

As Swami Vivekananda used to say, we are all beggars, always asking for more and more, and always unhappy. We are slaves to our desires. And even if we do get something, we feel it is not enough. We want more. We are never satisfied. But a person who has realized Brahman is happy. He says, 'I have everything.' The idea is, if you have attained the highest, the greatest, then worldly objects seem like trash to you. They may run after you, but you don't care for them.

Once Alexander the Great was trying to tempt an Indian yogi to come to Greece with him. But nothing could tempt the yogi. He had nothing of external things, but he had everything. He had Brahman. As the poem says, 'Having nothing, having all.' You may think: 'Oh, he was just a fool. He had nothing, yet he thought he had everything!' Yes, you may think he was a fool and that you are very wise and clever, but are you happy? Are you content?

Tat brahma iti upāsīta brahmavān bhavati. If you worship Brahman you become Brahman. Here the word *brahma* is used in the physical sense. You feel you are everywhere.

Brahmaṇaḥ parimara means Brahman's place of death. Śaṅkara says that this is space, since all natural phenomena—such as rain, lightning, the moon, the sun, and fire—disappear in space, as if this is where Brahman kills them.

Śaṅkara makes another interesting point. He says that when there is this sense of oneness, then who is the eater and what is it that is eaten? It is all one. You then turn away from this world of sense experience. Once Swami Vivekananda was making fun of the idea that everything is Brahman. Sri Ramakrishna just touched Swamiji and at once Swamiji saw Brahman in everything. He was in that state for several days, and during that time it was difficult for him to function. When he sat down to eat he saw that the food was Brahman and he himself was also Brahman, so how could he eat? When he walked in the street he saw that the carriages and other things were Brahman. Why should Brahman move out of the way of Brahman?

स य एवंवित्। अस्माल्लोकात्प्रेत्य। एतमन्नमयमात्मान-मुपसंक्रम्य। एतं प्राणमयमात्मानमुपसंक्रम्य। एतं मनोमय-मात्मानमुपसंक्रम्य। एतं विज्ञानमयमात्मानमुपसंक्रम्य। एत-मानन्दमयमात्मानमुपसंक्रम्य। इमाँल्लोकान्कामान्नी कामरू-प्यनुसंचरन्। एतत् साम गायन्नास्ते। हा३वु हा३वु हा३वु॥५॥

अहमन्नमहमन्नमहमन्नम्। अहमन्नादो३ऽहमन्नादो३ऽहम-न्नादः। अहꣳ श्लोककृदहꣳ श्लोककृदहꣳ श्लोककृत्। अहमस्मि प्रथमजा ऋता३स्य। पूर्वं देवेभ्योऽमृतस्य ना३भायि। यो मा ददाति स इदेव मा३ऽऽवाः। अहमन्न-मन्नमदन्तमा३द्मि। अहं विश्वं भुवनमभ्यभवा३म्। सुवर्न

ज्योतीः। य एवं वेद। इत्युपनिषत्॥६॥ इति दशमोऽनुवाकः॥

Sa ya evaṁvit; Asmāllokātpretya; Etamannamayam-ātmānamupasaṁkramya; Etaṁ prāṇamayamātmānam-upasaṁkramya; Etaṁ manomayamātmānamupasaṁ-kramya; Etaṁ vijñānamayamātmānamupasaṁkramya; Etamānandamayamātmānamupasaṁkramya; Imāṁllo-kānkāmānnī kāmarūpyanusaṁcaran; Etat sāma gāyan-nāste; Hā 3 vu hā 3 vu hā 3 vu.

Ahamannamahamannamahamannam; Ahamannādo 3-'hamannādo 3 'hamannādaḥ; Ahaṁ ślokakṛdahaṁ śloka-kṛdahaṁ ślokakṛt; Ahamasmi prathamajā ṛtā 3 sya; Pūrvaṁ devebhyo'mṛtasya nā 3 bhāyi; Yo mā dadāti sa ideva mā 3 ''vāḥ; Ahamannamannamadantamā 3 dmi; Ahaṁ viśvaṁ bhuvanamabhyabhavā 3 m; Suvarna jyotīḥ; Ya evaṁ veda; Ityupaniṣat. Iti daśamo'nuvākaḥ.

Saḥ yaḥ evaṁvit, he who knows this [i.e., who has attained the knowledge discussed earlier]; *asmāt lokāt,* from this world; *pretya,* having renounced; *etam annamayam ātmānam upasaṁkramya,* [first] identifying himself with the self represented by the body; *etam prāṇamayam ātmānam upasaṁkramya,* [next] identifying himself with the self represented by prāṇa, the vital breath; *etam manomayam ātmānam upasaṁkramya,* [then] identifying himself with the self represented by the mind; *etam vijñānamayam ātmānam upasaṁkramya,* identifying himself with the self represented by the intellect; [and finally] *etam ānanda-mayam ātmānam upasaṁkramya,* identifying himself with the self represented by bliss; *anusaṁcaran imān lokān kāmānnī* [i.e., *kāma* + *annī*] *kāmarūpī,* he goes about the three worlds choosing whatever 'anna' he likes and doing whatever he likes; *etat sāma gāyan āste,* filled with joy and astonishment at everything, he goes on singing; *hā-ā-ā-vu hā-ā-ā-vu hā-ā-ā-vu,* Oh! Oh! Oh!

Aham annam, I am food! [said thrice to emphasize astonishment]; *aham annādaḥ,* I am the eater of food! [said thrice for the same reason]; *aham ślokakṛt,* I am that which brings food and the eater together [producing thereby the living body] [said thrice, again for the same reason]; *aham prathamajāḥ ṛtasya asmi,* I am that which was born before anything [visible or invisible] in this world; *devebhyaḥ pūrvam,* I was born before the gods and goddesses; *amṛtasya nābhāyī,* [I am] the support of immortality; *yaḥ mā dadāti,* he who gives me [as food to someone who wants food]; *saḥ,* he; *it eva,* in this manner; *mā āvāḥ,* protects me; *annam adantam,* [if, on the other hand,] he does not give food to others; *aham annam admi,* I then eat him as if he is my food; *aham viśvam bhuvanam abhyabhavām,* I eat this whole world; *suvaḥ na jyotīḥ,* I always shine like the sun; *yaḥ evam veda,* he who knows this [gets the benefit already mentioned]; *iti upaniṣat,* this is the Upaniṣad. *Iti daśamaḥ anuvākaḥ,* here ends the tenth chapter.

5-6. He who has this knowledge [i.e., the knowledge of anna and annāda, food and the eater of food] has no interest whatsoever in this world of sense experience. He first thinks he is the body; next he identifies himself as prāṇa, the vital force; then he thinks he is the mind; next he identifies himself with the intellect; and following this, he identifies himself with ānanda, bliss. At this point he goes wherever he likes, choosing whatever he likes, and doing whatever he wants. He is full of Brahmānanda and expresses his joy and astonishment in words which hardly have any meaning: Oh! Oh! Oh! I am food, I am food, I am food! I am the eater, I am the eater, I am the eater! I bring together food and the eater of food and thereby create the living body. I am the first-born, being the predecessor of the world, both visible and invisible, and even of the gods and goddesses. I am the giver of liberation [i.e., immortality]. He who gives me as food to someone who needs food is then indirectly protecting me. But if someone, knowing me as food, does not give me away to a person who needs me, I may then eat him up myself. I swallow this whole world. I am as bright as the sun and I am self-effulgent. This is what is meant by the Upaniṣad. He who understands this Upaniṣad is rewarded as mentioned above.

Starting from the gross physical world (of food, annamaya) to the finest world (of bliss, ānandamaya), a person has to make a long journey. And the journey is not only long, it is also painful and difficult. But there is no escape from it if you want uninterrupted peace and happiness.

At the outset, a story is told of a young man, Bhṛgu, who approaches his scholarly father, Varuṇa, and asks for instructions about Brahman. Bhṛgu has to go back again and again to his father, each time being told by him that he must practise more austerities. Varuṇa goes to the extent of saying that austerities themselves constitute Brahman. This is like saying that the end and the means are the same. Given the means, the end follows automatically. If you remove the cover that hides a light, at once you can see the light. Similarly, if you remove your ego and all the hindrances it creates, the Self, which is always within you, will reveal itself with all its grandeur. What you need is a pure mind. And the one and only way to purify the mind is to practise austerities. This is why Varuṇa sends his son Bhṛgu back again and again, saying, 'Go and practise austerities.'

Bhṛgu did practise austerities. And each time he left his father, he came away with new inspiration in his heart and made more progress. For instance, he first thought he was the gross body (annamaya), but as he practised more austerities, he realized that he had a finer identity, which was that of the vital breath (prāṇamaya). Through austerities, he progressed from a finer to a still finer identity, and finally he attained his finest identity, which was bliss, the identity of Brahman. When a person realizes that he is one with Brahman, he has reached his goal. He then feels that not only is he Brahman but everything else is Brahman also. That is to say, there is only Brahman and nothing else. There is only one and that one is without a second.

But if there is only Brahman and nothing else, why has the concept of anna, food, and annāda, the eater, been brought in, which is dualistic? Why has this concept been posed at all when it is clearly contradictory to the proposition that all is one? How can 'many' be replaced by 'one'?

Śaṅkara explains that by virtue of austerities, duality is killed and a sense of oneness slowly grows in the mind. To begin with, anna and annāda seem to be different, but a close look at them will show that what is anna at one point is annāda at another point. Thus, the difference between them is only a matter of semantics. There is only one and that one appears to be many because of labels we use to suit our needs. Basically, all is one and one is all.

When you have this conviction, you are free from all biases of caste, creed, time, and place. You feel you are one with everything and everybody. All are one and the same to you. You are the happiest person on earth. When you reach that stage, you do not know how to express your joy. Your experience is beyond speech. You just laugh.

इति भृगुवल्ली समाप्ता ॥

Iti bhṛguvallī samāptā.

Here ends the Bhṛgu-vallī.

ॐ सह नाववतु। सह नौ भुनक्तु। सह वीर्यं करवावहै। तेजस्वि नावधीतमस्तु मा विद्विषावहै॥

ॐ शान्तिः शान्तिः शान्तिः॥

Om. Saha nāvavatu; Saha nau bhunaktu; Saha vīryaṁ karavāvahai; Tejasvi nāvadhītamastu mā vidviṣāvahai. Om Śāntiḥ Śāntiḥ Śāntiḥ.

May Brahman protect us both equally. May it also give us equally the benefit of the learning. May we both work equally hard to learn. May what we learn be equally fruitful. May we never be jealous of each other. Om Peace! Peace! Peace!